# Winning Presentation In A Day

# Winning Presentation In A Day

## Get it done right, get it done fast™

**Rhonda Abrams
and Guy Clapperton**

with Julie Vallone

CAPSTONE

Copyright © 2008 by Rhonda Abrams and Guy Clapperton

First published by
The Planning Shop™, a division of Rhonda, Inc., California corporation.
www.PlanningShop.com

This edition published by
Capstone Publishing Ltd. (a Wiley Company)
The Atrium, Southern Gate, Chichester, PO19 8SQ, UK.
www.wileyeurope.com
Email (for orders and customer service enquires): cs-books@wiley.co.uk

Other Wiley Editorial Offices
John Wiley & Sons Inc., 111 River Street, Hoboken, NJ 07030, USA
Jossey-Bass, 989 Market Street, San Francisco, CA 94103-1741, USA
Wiley-VCH Verlag GmbH, Boschstr. 12, D-69469 Weinheim, Germany
John Wiley & Sons Australia Ltd, 42 McDougall Street, Milton, Queensland 4064, Australia
John Wiley & Sons (Asia) Pte Ltd, 2 Clementi Loop #02-01, Jin Xing Distripark, Singapore 129809
John Wiley & Sons Canada Ltd, 22 Worcester Road, Etobicoke, Ontario, Canada M9W 1L1

Wiley also publishes its books in a variety of electronic formats. Some content that appears in print may not be available in electronic books.

A catalogue record for this book is available from the British Library.

ISBN 13: 978-1-84112-806-1

Printed and bound in Great Britain by TJ International Ltd, Padstow, Cornwall
Substantial discounts on bulk quantities of Capstone Books are available to corporations, professional associations and other organisations. For details telephone John Wiley & Sons on (+44) 1243-770441, fax (+44) 1243 770571 or email corporatedevelopment@ wiley.co.uk

# Winning Presentation In A Day

# Contents

# About the Authors

Rhonda Abrams is a syndicated columnist, best-selling author and popular public speaker. She has spent more than fifteen years advising, mentoring and consulting with entrepreneurs and small business owners. Her knowledge of the small business market and her passion for entrepreneurship have made her one of the USA's most recognised advocates for small business.

An experienced entrepreneur, Rhonda has started three successful companies, including a small business planning consulting firm. Her experience gives her a strong real-life understanding of the challenges facing entrepreneurs. Currently, she is the founder and CEO of The Planning Shop, a company focused on providing entrepreneurs with high-quality information and tools for developing successful businesses.

Guy Clapperton contributed regularly to the *Guardian*'s Business Sense section for small businesses throughout its eight-year run – as columnist, editorial associate and podcaster. Before this he ran a newsletter focusing on small business issues and continues to be fascinated by entrepreneurialism.

Currently, Guy writes business articles for the *Guardian*, *Financial Times*, *Esquire* and numerous other publications. He also writes for *The Times*, *The Sunday Times*, *Mail on Sunday*, *Independent*, *Radio Times* and other national publications. He broadcasts occasionally for BBC Radio London and the BBC World Service, normally about technology.

# The *In A Day* Promise
## Get it done right, get it done fast

**Y**ou're busy. We can help.

We are dedicated to helping entrepreneurs create and grow successful businesses. As entrepreneurs ourselves, we understand the many demands placed on you. We don't assume that you're a dummy, just that you're short on time.

This *In A Day* book will enable you to complete a critical business task in a hurry—and in the right way. You'll get it done right and get it done fast.

Can you complete this project in just twenty-four hours? Yes. Perhaps the twenty-four hours won't be consecutive. You may start—pause for an hour, day, or week to take care of other business—then return to the task later. Or, you may have some research or other preparation to do before you can complete this project.

We'll guide you through the process, show you what you absolutely have to do and give you tips and tricks to help you reach your goals. We've talked to the experts and done the research so you don't have to. We've also eliminated any unnecessary steps so you don't waste your valuable time. That's the *In A Day* promise.

When you have a business task you need to do *now*, the *In A Day* books will help you get it done—in as little as a day.

# Need a Winning Presentation Fast?

# This Book Is For You!

Do you have to give a presentation tomorrow—or next week? If you want yours to be a *winning presentation*, this book is for you!

Sooner or later, everyone has to give a presentation. In business, this might take the form of a sales call, a briefing to a department head, or a report to clients. Perhaps you've been asked to participate on a panel at a conference or to give a keynote speech. If you're presenting your business plan to investors, seeking a loan, or trying to land a major client, your company's future might depend on your presentation.

Presentations play key roles in other areas of life as well—from giving a report in class or leading a training session or retreat to speaking at a community organisation, church, synagogue, or mosque. If you have to speak to—and persuade—others, this book will help you succeed.

*Winning Presentation In A Day* was created for busy people like you. This guide provides you with the critical, time-tested tools and information you need to choose your content, create your message and pull together a well-constructed and effective presentation in record time.

*Winning Presentation In a Day* also includes valuable information on how to create an effective PowerPoint™ presentation. Whether you're new to PowerPoint, or are a power user who wants to add pizzazz to your presentations, this book shows you how to quickly and easily create slides that enhance your message and hold your listeners' attention.

Whatever your presentation goals, *Winning Presentation In A Day* gives you everything you need to get it done right—and get it done fast!

# Overview:
## What's a Presentation?

If you're like most people, you do presentations every day. Whenever you make a business phone call, attend a job interview, or enter a colleague's office for a discussion, you're presenting. A presentation is simply a conversation with an objective.

Granted, that's defining the word very loosely. A presentation is generally considered a more formal affair. It occurs at a certain place, focuses on a particular topic, is attended by an audience and takes place over a set period of time.

If it's a good presentation, it will be well organised and follow a thoughtful structure. Now, more than ever, it's likely to include visual aids and technology such as PowerPoint slides, projectors, microphones and other multimedia components.

If it's a *winning* presentation, it will persuade your listeners to share your point of view and you'll achieve your objectives.

Presenting is a skill you can learn and continually improve by knowing some simple techniques and understanding the most effective ways to choose and organise your content. Naturally, the more you present, the better you'll get!

## QUICK**TIP**

**Fear Factor**

Public speaking often tops polls as the thing business-people fear most – sometimes surpassing even death on the list of terrors! There can be a number of reasons – a history of under-delivery (usually due to overconfidence) is one, and a lack of practice. Business-people reason that if they can take decisions affecting a £mil-lion company every day they should be able to master a 15-minute presentation; they forget, however, that they face the business decisions every day, whereas they might get four or five cracks at business presentation per year.

You can, however, overcome your nerves. Millions of people do it every day – if they can do it, so can you!

## Why We Present

Presentations are a fact of business life. Even in an era entranced with high technology, one person talking in front of others is still a surprisingly popular and effective method of conveying information.

Presentations are given to:

- Make sales
- Clarify business strategies
- Inform others of new developments and data
- Share necessary business information
- Forge partnerships
- Create and enhance goodwill
- Increase team productivity
- Raise funds for new enterprises and projects
- Teach skills and behaviours
- Motivate and inspire
- Create consensus and agreement

No matter what your specific goal, this book will help you quickly put together a *winning presentation*—one that engages your audience, delivers your message and helps you achieve your aims.

*Winning Presentation In A Day* gives you the knowledge, tools and techniques to determine what to say, when to say it and how to say it well.

## Writing vs. Speaking

Have you ever gone to a meeting where a presenter stood before the audience and just read a research paper or article aloud? Chances are, you found your mind wandering or had trouble understanding the information. There's a reason: the skills used to understand a spoken presentation differ from those used to comprehend a written document. Effective presenters recognise this difference. People don't *read* presentations; they listen to them. Documents are created for the *eye,* while good presentations are created for the *ear.*

A presentation requires an audience to tune in for a limited period of time. The presenter has to effectively convey the message within that time. A document, by contrast, can usually be read at the reader's convenience. That means it can include far more detail or many more supporting arguments. A reader who doesn't understand a document the first time can go back and re-read it. In a presentation, your audience has to get the message the first—and only—time they hear it.

| DISTINCTIONS BETWEEN WRITTEN DOCUMENTS AND EFFECTIVE PRESENTATIONS | |
|---|---|
| **WRITTEN DOCUMENTS** | **WINNING PRESENTATIONS** |
| Can cover a number of topics | Clearly focus on a core message |
| Can be read and re-read until the reader understands them | Enable the audience to grasp the message the one and only time they hear it |
| Can build up slowly to make a point | Must catch the attention of an audience quickly |
| Can use many examples and subpoints | Select a limited number of powerful examples and subpoints |
| Can employ a large vocabulary and complex sentence structures | Use concise, easy-to-understand phrasing |
| The reader does not need to make a connection with the author | Establish a connection between the presenter and the audience |

# Using the Book

Throughout this book you'll see sample excerpts from a presentation by the fictional company ComputerEase. Next to these excerpts you'll find worksheets where you can jot down and organise information about your own presentation. By the time you finish each worksheet, you'll have all the information necessary for your own winning presentation.

The ComputerEase sample presentation sections illustrate how particular sections of a completed presentation might look. The sample excerpts are in an abbreviated form due to space limitations; your own presentation may be longer.

## COMPUTEREASE PRESENTATION TO WIDGET SOLUTIONS

**Presentation Category:** Sales
**Focus On:** What we want audience to *do*—use ComputerEase's services
**Presentation Goals:** To convince Widget's Human Resources department to sign up for a trial training programme and use ComputerEase's training services exclusively in the future

Use the worksheets to write down the information you'll need to complete your own presentation. If there's not enough space on the worksheets, use a separate piece of paper to record your thoughts and data.

---

**Use this worksheet to list your own presentation category, focus and goals.**

What kind of presentation will you be making?

What do you want your audience to think, do, feel, or remember?

What are the goals of your presentation?

# How to
## Use This Book

To create *Winning Presentation In A Day*, we gleaned the most useful information from the people who know the subject best. We turned to those who do presentations for a living—professional speakers, corporate managers and speech coaches. We even consulted the PowerPoint specialists at Microsoft's corporate headquarters.

Drawing from this vast body of knowledge, *Winning Presentation In A Day* outlines the key elements of an effective presentation in a step-by-step guide. Within each step, you'll find the tools you need to help you create your own winning presentation, including:

- QuickTips with insiders' secrets for making your presentation even more effective
- Checklists outlining what you'll accomplish in each step
- Lists of 'Time-Saving Tools' showing what information to have handy to speed your task
- Worksheets to help you gather and organise the content for your presentation
- A sample business presentation showing you exactly how a successful presentation is pulled together, from start to finish

In the first sections of *Winning Presentation In A Day*, you'll learn how to select and organise your content. You'll also create your core message, choose your major arguments and define your call to action.

In the sections that follow, you'll discover how to improve your delivery style and manage audience interaction. You'll also learn tricks for overcoming stage fright.

The final three sections are devoted to creating PowerPoint presentations. These sections include:

- **Getting Started with PowerPoint:** a guide for those who have never, or rarely, used PowerPoint or want guidance on PowerPoint basics
- **Slide Rules:** expert insight on how to make your slides most effective
- **Enhancing Your PowerPoint Presentation:** tips, tricks and instructions for adding punch to your presentation

From the step-by-step guidelines for building a presentation, to the valuable insights from our experts, *Winning Presentation In A Day* is your one-stop resource for creating a successful presentation. Our goal: to help you get your winning presentation finished, get it done right and get it done fast.

# 1

**STEP 1: Gather the Details**

## Accomplishments

*In this step you'll:*

- ☐ 1. Focus on the topic of your presentation
- ☐ 2. Select a title for your presentation
- ☐ 3. Find out what type of presentation you'll be giving
- ☐ 4. Learn what type of audience you'll be presenting to
- ☐ 5. Find out the size of your audience
- ☐ 6. Learn how much time you'll have for your presentation and any Q&A
- ☐ 7. Find out where you'll be giving the presentation and what the room will be like
- ☐ 8. Discover what equipment will be available
- ☐ 9. Gather any other critical information

## Time-Saving Tools

*You'll complete this step more quickly if you have any of the following handy:*

- ☐ 1. Your event organiser's name and contact information
- ☐ 2. A list of the equipment you'll use in your presentation

# Step One:
## Gather the Details

**QUICKTIP**

**Surprise!**

Some event organisers don't plan—or communicate—critical details until the last minute. That means you may arrive for your presentation to discover you've got five minutes instead of an hour to speak, 20 people in your audience instead of 200, or that there's no LCD projector for your PowerPoint presentation. Keep the worksheet on page 19 in front of you and call your event contact well in advance of your presentation. You'll help them get better organised and keep yourself from being unpleasantly surprised.

Who will you be speaking to? About what? When? Before you develop and organise the content of your presentation, you must first gather some key logistical details.

Some of these details may seem basic. But they will affect your choice of content, organisation, delivery and timing. Knowing exactly what you'll face during your presentation will save you time, build your confidence and help you avoid unexpected glitches.

The basic presentation details you need to know:

- Topic
- Title
- Type of presentation
- Type of audience
- Size of audience
- Time
- Location
- Equipment
- Other critical information

You should be able to get all this information by making a telephone call to your presentation contact. Don't send an email; you'll get a better feel for the nature of the event and the group you'll be speaking to by actually chatting with an event organiser.

# 1. Topic

Few people will ever invite you to speak and then ask, 'What are you going to talk about?' After all, the reason you've been asked to present—or you've asked for the opportunity to present—is that you have knowledge to share with an audience.

In most cases, you'll be assigned a specific topic at the time you're asked to speak. You may be asked to participate in a panel discussion on your company's approach to marketing, you might be part of a team reporting on third quarter results, or you could have been invited to speak to an organisation about new developments in your industry.

Of course, there are also times when there seems to be no 'topic'. For instance, there isn't usually a topic announced when you're giving a sales presentation to a prospective client. Nevertheless, it's up to you to focus on a specific issue. During a sales presentation, the topic may be your company's new products and their benefits to your prospect.

The key to an effective presentation is to clearly understand your topic and then focus on the specific aspects of that topic most relevant to your audience.

When determining which aspects of your topic to centre on, consider:

- What does your audience want to know about your topic? What do they care about most? What aspects of your topic have an impact on their lives and businesses?

- How much information do listeners want on the topic? What level of detail will they expect? What's their attention span?

- What specific information do you want your audience to walk away with? What should they leave your presentation knowing, believing, or prepared to do?

## 2. Title

Even when you are assigned a topic for your presentation, you'll often be given the chance, or responsibility, to come up with a title. But how do you come up with a snazzy title for a presentation on third quarter results?

The safest and easiest way to select a title is to choose a simple descriptive phrase: *'Third Quarter Results'*. This isn't snazzy, but it makes clear what you're going to be talking about.

Of course, a straightforward title isn't necessarily going to encourage people to attend, or look forward to, your presentation. They may be yawning before they even enter the room.

Instead, try to find a title that gives your presentation some personality. A few ways to do this:

- **Title/subtitle**: Come up with a positive or inviting title and a descriptive subtitle or vice versa. *'Beating Expectations: Third Quarter Results'* or *'Third Quarter Results: Beating Expectations'*

- **Work in a positive word or phrase:** Listeners are attracted to upbeat information or advice: *'Growth!'*

- **Use numbers:** Using numbers gives you a framework for organising your presentation: *'Seven Sure-fire Ways to Close a Sale'*

- **Promise usefulness:** Audiences are particularly interested in information that will help them accomplish something. Combine this promise with positive words and/or numbers: *'Six Easy Ways to Increase Website Traffic'*

- **Promise completeness:** It's appealing to learn a lot in a short amount of time: *'Buying Your First Home, from A–Z'*

- **Use the unexpected:** It can be intriguing to turn a title upside down or provide an unusual approach to your topic: *'Six Sure-Fire Ways to* Lose *a Sale'*

- **Offer detail:** When speaking to a knowledgeable audience, a title reflecting detail indicates they'll learn something substantive: *'Process-Based Auditing Required by ISO 9001:2000'*

- **Be catchy, not corny:** It's OK to be a little bit corny, just make sure you're not *too* contrived for your audience: *'Bytes into Bites: Generating Sales Leads from Your Website'*

When choosing a title, keep in mind the venue and audience for your presentation. At a scientific conference, for instance, a clever title may be frowned upon. And truthfully, a department report on third quarter results doesn't require a very exciting title.

# 3. Type of presentation

The type of presentation you'll be giving will affect virtually every other choice you make about it. Even if you always speak about the same topic, a difference in presentation type can change the content you choose as well as the way you organise and deliver it.

Let's say you've been asked to speak on your company's new marketing programmes. If you were giving a twenty-minute keynote speech, you'd concentrate on the big picture and work on motivating your listeners to use the programmes. In a two-hour workshop, you'd give your audience step-by-step instructions on how to implement them. During a five-minute segment on a panel discussion about marketing, you'd limit yourself to touting the benefits of one specific programme.

The single most important thing to know is whether you'll be speaking alone or on a panel with others. As a lone speaker, whether for a keynote speech, workshop, or sales pitch, you've got a lot more control over what to say and how to say it. If you're to be a panel member, your event organiser will typically tell you exactly what to address. And you'll generally be given a lot less time to address it. So your choices about what to say and how to say it will be limited.

As you begin to develop your presentation, keep in mind the format, or type, of presentation you've been asked to give.

# Keynote Speech

**Why:** Goals vary; this kind of presentation can be informational, persuasive, inspirational, entertainment-oriented, or used to set a tone or theme for a conference

**Who:** One person to a large audience; typically, the audience will be individuals from an industry trade group, employees of a company, or members of an association or organisation

**Where:** Conference or convention centre or a hotel equipped with large meeting facilities

**Timing:** Fifteen minutes to one hour; may take place during a meal

**Keys to Success:** Concentrate on overall themes rather than small details; maintain high energy level; if possible, add an element of motivation, inspiration, or entertainment; use microphone and audiovisual (AV) equipment

# Seminar/Workshop

**Why:** Education and/or skills development

**Who:** One or more persons present to a small- or medium-sized group, usually made up of professionals in a particular field or members of an association

**Where:** Venues vary widely, from small company meeting rooms to larger conference rooms

**Timing:** Forty-five minutes to all day; may be a break-out session at a larger conference

**Keys to Success:** Provide specific details about the topic, since the audience is there to learn; concentrate on helpful information; provide handouts; include an interactive element, if possible

# Panel Discussion

**Why:** To present different perspectives on one topic or issue

**Who:** Several topic experts share their views with (and answer questions from) a medium to large audience; a moderator takes questions

**Where:** Varies by size of panel and audience, but usually occurs in a medium to large conference room

**Timing:** Each panel member is usually given five to twenty minutes to speak; additional time is allowed for questions and answers (Q&A)

**Keys to Success:** Speak to other panel members to learn what they're discussing before planning your presentation; when speaking, focus on a limited number of points

# Report

**Why:** To update others in your company—or to report to clients—on a variety of matters, including work in progress, strategies, research findings, new policies and financial matters

**Who:** One or more employees or consultants presents to colleagues or clients; typically a small group

**Where:** Typically on company's premises; usually in conference room

**Timing:** Five minutes to a few hours, depending on the nature of report and number of presenters

**Keys to Success:** Know exactly who will be in the room and understand their key concerns; provide supporting material; be clear as to whether this is an information-only or action-directed report

---

## QUICK**TIP**

### Panel Preparation

If you are asked to speak as part of a panel, you'll want to ask the event organiser:

- How many members will be on the panel and who they are

- What topics—or aspect of the topics—the other panel members will be discussing

- How much time each of you will have

- Who the moderator will be

- Will there be a Q&A, and if so will it be individual or to the panel as a whole

- Contact information for other panel members and the moderator, if desired

## Sales Pitch/Product Demonstration

**Why:** To sell a product or service to a customer or potential customer

**Who:** One or more salespeople or company personnel present to one customer or many representatives of a client company

**Where:** Typically at customer's premises; usually in conference room, office, or work area

**Timing:** Five minutes to one hour; typically broken up by client questions

**Keys to Success:** Focus on benefits to customer; anticipate questions and be prepared with answers

## Business Plan Presentation

**Why:** To secure financing for a business from investors or lenders

**Who:** Can involve as few as two people (a business founder presenting to an angel investor or bank lender), or many people (a management team presenting to a roomful of venture capitalists)

**Where:** Typically at the investor's or lender's office; can also take place on company premises; usually in conference room; could take place at a conference centre if presenting to a large group of potential investors

**Timing:** Fifteen minutes to one hour; typically broken up by client's questions

**Keys to Success:** Concentrate on your company's key strategic advantages and the potential return on your audience's investment; anticipate questions and be prepared with answers

# Motivational or Inspirational Speech

**Why:** To inspire or persuade an audience, entertain, or generate goodwill

**Who:** One person before a large audience; typically attendees at a convention or at a public event

**Where:** Conference or convention centre or hotel equipped with large meeting facilities

**Timing:** Fifteen minutes to one hour; may be delivered during a meal

**Keys to Success:** Concentrate on larger themes rather than specific details; include inspirational stories or examples; give emphasis to aspects of the topic with an emotional appeal

# Web Conference/Audio Conference/ Video Conference

**Why:** To share information, instruct, or persuade

**Who:** One or more people presenting to a number of geographically dispersed participants

**Where:** On the phone and/or on the Internet; in a video-conferencing centre

**Timing:** Thirty minutes to a few hours

**Keys to Success:** Distribute supporting information (data, reports, visuals) in advance of conference; recognise that attendees may become distracted or deal with other matters during the presentation, so concentrate on supplying key information quickly

## 4. Type of audience

Who will be attending your presentation? What are their jobs or positions? How much do they know about the subject? What are they likely to be interested in learning?

When you know who's in your audience, it's easier to shape a more effective and compelling presentation.

When assessing the makeup of your audience try to learn:

- **Is it a specific group or a general audience?** Is your audience made up of a specific group with an industry, job responsibilities, or goals in common? Or is yours a more diverse audience, with a variety of backgrounds, goals and interests? It's easier to tailor your content when you're speaking to a group with similar characteristics.

- **Why are they attending?** What do the members of the audience hope to get out of your presentation? Do they want to gather specific information, learn new techniques, stay informed about new developments, or be motivated? Are they attending willingly or is this a job requirement? Have they paid to be there? Are there any political disagreements or office politics that may affect your presentation?

- **What is their level of knowledge?** Are all your listeners well acquainted with the topic or is this new to them? Are they looking for a general overview of the topic or specific details? Remember, even if everyone in your audience is from the same industry or works at the same company, they may have different levels of understanding. You'll have a much better sense of how to present your topic if you ask your event organiser to estimate the experience and knowledge level of your listeners.

- **Will any cultural factors come into play?** This is particularly relevant if you're presenting in a foreign country or to a culturally diverse audience. How well does your audience speak and understand English? Are they comfortable with presentations that include audience interaction, or would they prefer not to participate?

- **What other audience demographic factors should you consider?** You may choose to tailor your presentation's style or content to the demographic makeup of your listeners. Your presentation may be more informal and faster-paced when you're speaking to a group in their twenties than it would be when addressing an older group.

# 5. Size of audience

How many people will be attending your presentation? The size of your audience will influence such aspects of your presentation as:

- Style/level of formality

- Interactivity

- How you take questions

- Use of audiovisual equipment

You can be a lot more informal when addressing a small group than when presenting to a large audience. For example, you can include more personal experiences as part of your content or even ask listeners to share their experiences. However, there may be times when even a small group requires a more formal style. Let's say you're presenting your business plan to a group of venture capitalists (VCs) for funding. Whether you're speaking to 3, 30, or 300 VCs, you'll want to deliver a *very* well-rehearsed presentation, complete with PowerPoint™ slides, and avoid casual comments about your personal life.

# 6. Time

QUICK**TIP**

**Timing Is Everything**

The best way to figure out how long your presentation will take is to practise it a few times, using a timer. Keep in mind that when you actually give your presentation, you are likely to speed up. If you write out your presentation, a rule of thumb used by many presenters is that it takes about two minutes to deliver one double-spaced typewritten page.

Ask how much time you'll have to speak. Once you know whether you're giving a seven-minute panel presentation, a one-hour speech, or an all-day workshop, you'll be better equipped to choose and organise your content. Practice your presentation using a timer. Plan your coverage so it fits the time slot.

Find out how much time you are expected to leave for questions from the audience. Be clear about whether the time for questions is in addition to the time you'll be given to speak or whether it should be carved out from your total presentation time.

Of course, there will always be situations where, at the last moment, you'll be given less (or more) time than promised. To prepare for the unexpected, consider in advance how you could cut your presentation if necessary—and have additional material ready in case you're given additional time.

When will you be giving your presentation? You need to know this so you can show up on time (and make travel arrangements if you're coming from out of town). When constructing your presentation—particularly your opening—you might also want to consider what time of day you'll be appearing. Audiences generally have more energy in the morning than they do immediately after lunch. If you are scheduled to present after lunch, add an element of audience interaction, like a quiz or demonstration, to keep listeners attentive and involved.

# 7. Location

Gather information about the venue, room size and room arrangement before you arrive to give your presentation.

Ask your event organiser:

● Where will the presentation take place?

● How large is the space?

● Will the audience be seated in chairs or at tables? How will the room be arranged?

● Where will you be in relation to the audience? Will you present from a stage?

● Will you be able to interact with or move around the audience?

Feel free to tell the event organisers what type of room arrangement you'd prefer or where you'd like to stand in relation to the audience.

Arrive early to see the place you'll be giving your presentation. You'll discover that the room arrangements often differ from what was originally promised. If it's an informal or small venue, don't be afraid to ask for, or make, some simple changes, such as rearranging the chairs.

## 8. Equipment

Few things are more distressing to a presenter who's slaved over a PowerPoint presentation than to arrive at a venue and discover that the room is not equipped with a projector or screen. It's critical to know what types of AV equipment will be available before you begin creating your presentation.

You'll also want to know what other equipment is available for use, such as microphones, pointers, video, or other multimedia equipment.

Ask your event contact:

● Will there be a projector and screen for a PowerPoint presentation? Do you need to bring cables to link your computer in?

● Should you bring your own computer or will there be a computer available for your presentation? If so, will you need to email your PowerPoint presentation in advance or bring it on disk?

● Will there be a microphone? If so, what type (lapel/radio mike, fixed to podium, hand-held)?

● What other equipment will be available or will be used?

● If you are conducting a Web, audio, or video conference, be sure to get full instructions about accessing the system, speaking and answering questions, and sharing visuals. See if you can do a few run-throughs in advance with the meeting planners.

# 9. Other critical information

Other information that may be important as you plan your presentation:

● **Nature and schedule of the event.** If your presentation is part of a larger event (such as a conference or convention), be certain to get the details for and schedule of the complete event. This gives you a much better sense of the context of your presentation and the other presentations your audience will hear.

● **Deadlines.** Your event coordinator may want you to submit various items in advance of your presentation, including your bio, presentation title, a presentation outline, copies of your PowerPoint slides and handouts. Be certain to ask for the deadlines for sending any required material.

● **Handouts.** Will you be passing out any worksheets or information to attendees? If so, is it your responsibility to make copies or will the event organiser do this?

● **Other events you're expected to attend.** Occasionally presenters may be invited to, or expected to, attend other functions that are part of an event. (This is especially true at conferences and conventions). Ask your event contact whether this will be the case for you.

# Pulling It All Together: Gather the Details

You'll be a lot more confident if you know as much as you can about your audience and the event well ahead of your presentation. The small amount of time it takes to contact the event organiser to ask about basic details will pay off the day you stand in front of your audience.

It's worth it to do a little extra investigation before any presentation, especially about your audience. The more you know about the needs and interests of your listeners, the better you'll be able to tailor your content to make it particularly relevant and appealing. Check out websites, news articles and marketing studies relating to your audience.

Try to arrive early. Take a look at the room setup. Check to make sure all the equipment is working. If you can, strike up conversations with people who will be attending. Find out what they're looking for, what problems they're trying to resolve and what they expect to hear. These simple steps may result in a few minor presentation adjustments that could make a world of difference.

On the next pages you'll find the details for a presentation to be given by Susan Alexander, the director of marketing of the fictional company ComputerEase. Use the worksheet on the pages that follow to gather the details for your own presentation.

## COMPUTEREASE PRESENTATION TO WIDGET SOLUTIONS

**Meeting contact:** Zoe Green, PA to HR director Geraldine McFry

**Phone number:** 555-1324

**Topic:** ComputerEase's training services, benefits and savings to clients

**Title:** ComputerEase: FastTrack to Success

**Type of presentation:** Sales Pitch

**Purpose of presentation:** To introduce the Widget Solutions human resources team to ComputerEase's programmes and to convince them to sign up for a trial on-site class.

**Audience:** Senior-level Widget Solutions HR personnel

**Number in audience:** 6

**Why they are attending:** To find an effective computer training programme that saves money and improves skill sets. Widget's HR has been under pressure to cut costs in the company and reduce the need for outside IT support. Widget management is currently investigating competitors' services.

**How much they already know:** They have limited technical knowledge; their primary concern is their budget

**Time available:** 45 minutes, including Q&A

**Location:** Widget Solutions office

**Room:** Company conference room, about 300 square feet. Oval conference table.

**Equipment to be used:** ComputerEase's laptop; Widget's projector and screen

**Other information:** Handouts to be left with audience

Inquired about facility in advance

**Use this form when interviewing your presentation organiser or contact, or for your own presentation research notes.**

Who is your event contact?

What is this person's contact information?

What is the topic of your presentation?

What is the title of your presentation?

What type of presentation will you be giving?

Why are you giving this presentation?

Who will be in your audience?

How many audience members will there be?

Why are they attending your presentation?

How much does your audience already know about the topic?

_____

_____

How much time will you have for your presentation (without a question-and-answer period)?

_____

_____

How much time is available for Q&A?

_____

_____

Where will your presentation take place? (Geographical location)

_____

_____

What kind of room will it be in? How will the room be set up?

_____

_____

What equipment do you plan to use?

_____

_____

What equipment is available?

_____

_____

Is there any other critical information (schedules, deadlines, handouts) you need to be aware of?

_____

_____

_____

_____

_____

**2**

## Accomplishments

*In this step you'll:*

- ☐ 1. Identify the purpose and goals of your presentation
- ☐ 2. Learn how to make your presentation matter to an audience
- ☐ 3. Identify your core message
- ☐ 4. Learn how your main supporting arguments strengthen your core message
- ☐ 5. Understand how subpoints enhance your supporting arguments
- ☐ 6. Identify your call to action
- ☐ 7. Learn how to thank your audience

## Time-Saving Tools

*You'll complete this step more quickly if you have any of the following handy:*

- ☐ 1. Information about why your audience is attending your presentation
- ☐ 2. Information about your audience's area of expertise
- ☐ 3. Information about the knowledge level of your audience
- ☐ 4. A clear idea of what you want your audience to do, feel, think, or remember after your presentation is over

# Step 2:
## Content

**QUICKTIP**

**It's All About** *Them*

Why are your listeners there? As you develop your content, think about the specific needs, problems and issues that motivated them to attend your presentation. Make it clear that you're there to address their concerns, propose a solution, or improve their lives. Audiences perk up when they know there's something in it for them. When you think about what the audience wants to hear, not just what you want to say, your presentation is more likely to be a winning one.

Your delivery might be superb, your PowerPoint slides stunning, but none of that will matter if you don't have clear and compelling content. It's your content that convinces your audience to share your point of view and motivates them to take action.

When you get up in front of a room, you're the expert. But that doesn't mean you have to know absolutely *everything* there is to know about the topic you'll be presenting on. After all, you were asked—or you requested the opportunity—to give a presentation because you have information to share with your audience.

If you're to speak before an industry conference, the event planner chose you because of your knowledge of that industry. If you're giving a report on a project, you've probably been working on it for some time. And if you're giving a sales or product demonstration, it's a good bet that you know a lot more about your product or service than your audience.

So relax; you almost never need to go out and do a lot of research to prepare for a presentation. Since you're already well informed about your subject, the key issue when it comes to content is deciding what to include and what to leave out.

When you begin to select your content, to choose what's important and what's not, it's essential to know three things:

- Why you're giving the presentation

- How you can make your presentation matter to the audience

- What you want your audience to remember after the presentation is over

Once you know these things, it will be easier to focus on the three key components of any winning presentation:

- Your core message

- Your supporting arguments

- Your call to action

# 1. Why are you giving this presentation?

What do you hope to achieve by giving your presentation? A winning presentation has a clear purpose and goals.

Most presenters, however, never really focus on their goals. They just know they have to show up at a certain place and speak for a particular amount of time. It's no wonder that their presentations fail to make much of an impact on their audience.

Think about whether you want to explain new procedures to your department, win support for a policy change, make a sale, increase industry awareness of your products, or attract financing for your business. Perhaps your aim is to make your audience feel good about your company or about themselves. Defining your goal will make it easier for you to devise a plan for achieving it.

Use the chart opposite along with the sample and worksheet below to clarify your presentation goals.

## COMPUTEREASE PRESENTATION TO WIDGET SOLUTIONS

**Presentation Category:** Sales

**Focus On:** What we want audience to *do*—Use ComputerEase's services

**Presentation Goals:** To convince Widget's human resources department to sign up for a trial training programme and use ComputerEase's training services exclusively in the future

---

**Use this worksheet to list your own presentation category, focus and goals.**

What kind of presentation will you be making?

What do you want your audience to think, do, feel, or remember?

What are the goals of your presentation?

| PRESENTATION CATEGORY | FOCUS ON | PRESENTATION GOALS | EXAMPLES |
|---|---|---|---|
| **Informational/ Instructional** | What you want your audience to *think* | Build understanding of your topic or teach your audience new skills | Explaining a new company policy<br><br>Detailing the provisions of a health plan<br><br>Reporting on the progress of a project<br><br>Teaching staff how to use a new computer programme, or new sales techniques |
| **Persuasive/ Sales** | What you want your audience to *do* | Convince your audience to act on a problem using your solution | Meeting with bankers or investors to finance a business<br><br>Attempting to win support for a new company strategy or policy<br><br>Convincing prospective customers to do business with you |
| **Motivational/ Inspirational** | What you want your audience to *feel* | Motivate your audience to adopt a new approach or attitude, and act accordingly<br><br>Make them feel good about themselves | Giving a pep talk at company retreat<br><br>Speaking at a year-end banquet for non-profit organisation<br><br>Being a motivational speaker at industry convention |
| **Goodwill/ Promotional** | What you want your audience to *remember* | Build credibility and reputation of your company or organisation | Participating on a panel presentation highlighting your company's innovations<br><br>Talking to prospective employees on company benefits and culture<br><br>Giving a presentation showcasing a corporation's community involvement |

## QUICK**TIP**

**Bring It Home**

Tie some of your content to information that resonates with your audience. Connect with your listeners by mentioning:

- **Current events.** Are there any recent events that make your presentation particularly timely?

- **Geographic connections.** Are there any local or regional tie-ins to your topic that could demonstrate that your content relates to listeners where they live?

- **Industries.** Can you demonstrate how your content applies to an audience's industry or business?

- **Departments.** Are there any aspects of your topic that have specific implications for their department?

## 2. How can you make your presentation matter to an audience?

Listeners pay a lot more attention to a presentation when they can relate to the content. As you develop your presentation, include information that hits home with your audience. Use examples, data, or an opening hook (see page 43) that reflects their day-to-day reality.

This is especially important when you're speaking to a group of people you don't come into contact with every day, such as those in other companies, industries, communities, or even other departments.

Let's say you're an expert on direct-mail marketing, and you've been asked to speak to a group of bed-and-breakfast owners. During your presentation, include examples of other bed-and-breakfast owners who have used direct mail successfully. Your audience will feel like you are speaking directly to them and understand the issues they face. This technique will make your presentation more powerful than if you had only talked in general terms about direct mail.

## Areas of Responsibility

Your presentation will be most effective if you focus on the specific aspects of the topic that relate to your audience's *area of responsibility.*

Imagine you're in charge of the relaunch of your company's website. You've been involved with every element of the website's design and development, and you could speak about any part of it. However, what you choose to include in a presentation about the site will depend on who you're speaking to.

It's easy to become focused on the issues that most concern you, or that you think are most interesting, rather than homing in on the content that is of most interest and importance to your audience. You may feel that the most exciting part of developing your website was using a new software language, but few of the sales reps will care.

## Level of Expertise

As you choose your content, keep in mind your listeners' level of expertise. The more experienced and knowledgeable they are, the more information you can provide.

You can offer more programming details about the online ordering process to the tech department than you could to the marketing personnel.

A challenge arises when audience members have widely divergent levels of expertise. In most groups, but especially in large groups, some listeners will have far more knowledge about the topic than others.

When that is the case, first try to determine the knowledge level of those members of the audience who are *most* important to you. For instance, if you're giving a report to a group chaired by the CEO, tailor your talk to her level of expertise, even if everyone in the room knows a lot less about website development than she does.

When everyone in the audience is important, the safest path is to choose a middle ground, aiming your content at the majority of those in attendance. Be sure to ask your event organiser about the knowledge level of the attendees when you plan your presentation.

Use the sample and worksheet on page 29 to help tailor your content to your audience.

# Match Your Content to Your Audience

What you'll say about the relaunch of your company's website will change depending on who you're presenting to, how much they already know about it and what's important to them. Always keep your *audience's* needs and interests in mind when choosing content for your presentation.

| AUDIENCE | CONTENT |
| --- | --- |
| **Your company's marketing department** | The website's visual design, the ways the new site attracts and retains customers, and how you'll increase traffic to the site |
| **Sales department** | The ways products or services are merchandised, orders are taken and commissions are tracked |
| **Tech department** | The technical aspects of the site, hardware and software, and the ongoing tech maintenance the site needs |
| **Company executives** | How the site improves the company's overall image, the total costs of development and the impact on the bottom line |
| **An industry association** | The challenges of launching a website for a company like yours. |
| **A professional web developers group** | Specific technical challenges of launching the website |

## COMPUTEREASE PRESENTATION TO WIDGET SOLUTIONS

**The audience is here because:** Widget Systems is spending too much money on outside technical support and is looking for ways to reduce this cost by educating staff on how to deal with the problems themselves.

**Tie-ins to audience:** Mention the £520,000 they spent last year on emergency tech support.

**Their area of responsibility:** Human resources

**They already know:** About budget and staffing issues

**They are most interested in:** Saving money and reducing the number of work hours lost to computer problems

**They are least interested in:** The technical details about what causes computer problems

---

**Use this worksheet to fill in details that will help you make your presentation matter to your audience.**

Why is my audience attending?

Are there any tie-ins to the topic (current events, industry news) that my audience can relate to?

What is their area of responsibility?

How much do they already know about my topic?

What's of most interest to them?

What's of least interest?

## QUICK**TIP**

**Won't It Get Boring?**

Since you're going to repeat your core message a number of times throughout your presentation, you may be concerned that you'll bore your audience. That's unlikely. It takes many repetitions before a message will sink in.

# 3. Core message

What do you want your listeners to remember? If a reporter were to ask someone leaving your presentation what they had learned, what would you want them to say?

You'd want them to remember—and repeat—your core message. If all your audience walks away with is that one crucial sentence, your presentation will have been a success.

Most presenters don't have, or can't identify, a core message. During their presentations they recite facts or give the audience detail after detail about a process or service. They serve up too much information for listeners to digest. When they're done, listeners don't know what conclusion they are supposed to reach. When a presentation lacks a core message, its audience lacks direction.

Think of your core message as you would the tagline for your business—it's a one-line statement that sums up the most important aspect of your presentation. You'll repeat it a number of times throughout your talk.

An effective core message is:

- **Clear**. It contains one unmistakable central theme, unclouded by other ideas.

- **Concise.** It's short, powerful and to the point.

- **Memorable**. It remains fixed in the minds of your audience.

- **Important to your audience**. They can understand how your message affects them or can identify with others it impacts.

- **Convincing**. If your message is persuasive, your audience will take the action you recommend.

QUICK**TIP**

Strong core messages make clear what you want your audience to think, feel, remember, or do. Weak core messages fail to lead listeners to a conclusion.

Let's say you're giving a sales presentation to a prospective client:

- **Weak core message:** This is what our company does.

- **Strong core message:** Use our company and save money.

Or you're giving a presentation about the good work done by the RSPCA (Royal Society for the Prevention of Cruelty to Animals):

- **Weak core message:** Here are some programmes we have to help animals.

- **Strong core message:** Your donations save animals' lives.

Or, you've been asked to give a report on third quarter results:

- **Weak core message:** Here are our third quarter results.

- **Strong core message:** Our team achieved the best third quarter in company history.

Remember: Your core message is the heart of your presentation. It will be the foundation for everything else you say. Make sure every other element of your presentation supports it, enhances it and makes it memorable to your listeners.

**Staying 'On Message'**

Politicians, successful ones at least, are notorious for staying 'on message'. Before they appear in public or have TV microphones shoved in their faces, they've worked out a short, pithy message, and no matter what question they're asked, they somehow find a way to include it in their response. While this frustrates broadcasters—and many voters—the constant repetition of a core message helps them set themselves apart from other candidates with different messages and lets the public know who they are and what they're all about in a very few words.

## COMPUTEREASE PRESENTATION TO WIDGET SOLUTIONS

**Core Message:** The unique training programme developed and tested by ComputerEase will save Widget money.

**What's your core message?**

# 4. Main supporting arguments

How will you convince your audience to accept your core message? What makes it memorable and convincing?

Once you've selected a core message, you've got to explain to your audience why they should believe and agree with you—and take the action you request.

Supporting arguments exist to make the case for why your listeners should believe your core message and act as you suggest. In most presentations, especially those more than five or ten minutes long, the arguments that support your core message will make up the bulk of what you say— at least in terms of how much time you spend discussing them. But keep in mind these supporting arguments are not the key information you want your audience to remember or act on—your core message is.

To make your arguments convincing, choose evidence that will have the most impact on your listeners and that is most likely to overcome their disbelief or hesitation. This includes:

- Verifiable examples
- Statistics/data
- Documented facts
- Published studies and research
- Testimonials
- Case studies
- Convincing reasons

Let's say you want to persuade management that it's time to find a new location for your company. Your core message is 'We need a new facility now.' Three strong supporting arguments:

- We have more employees than the building can hold
- Our current infrastructure can't handle our technology needs
- Our growth is being stifled by our lack of room to expand

For more on main supporting arguments, see pages 46, 48 and 49.

# 5. Subpoints that support your main arguments

Depending on the time allotted for your presentation, you may be able to add subpoints to give your main arguments more of a punch. These subpoints help prove or support the contention you make in your main arguments.

Once again, the types of information to include in your subpoints are:

- Verifiable examples

- Statistics/data

- Documented facts

- Published studies and research

- Testimonials

- Case studies

- Convincing reasons

So if you're trying to convince management that it's time to find a new location, here are the types of subpoints you could add to one of your main supporting arguments:

**Main argument:** We have more employees than the building can hold.

**Subpoints:**

a) Our current facility was built for 150 and we now employ 250

b) Three out of every five managers currently share an office or cubicle

c) In a recent survey taken by HR, employees said overcrowding was the number one reason for low morale

You don't have to provide subpoints for every major argument. But when you have the time—and the information—including them can make an even stronger case for your position.

But don't overwhelm your listeners. In general, follow the 'Rule of Three': offer no more than three main supporting arguments in any presentation and no more than three subpoints to support any main argument. (For more on the Rule of Three, see page 46.)

For more on subpoints, see pages 47, 48 and 49.

## 6. Call to action

Now that you've convinced your listeners that your core message is supported by strong and convincing evidence, you must let them know what you want them to do.

In most cases, you'll want your listeners to behave differently after they've heard your presentation. You may want them to buy your product, support your proposal, or feel better about your company.

But while you may believe it's obvious what they should do, think, remember or feel after your presentation, your audience may not draw the same conclusion. So you've got to let them know exactly what it is that you'd like from them. You've got to give them a *call to action*.

Your call to action will appear in the closing portion of your presentation. The call to action points your audience in a particular direction. It can be:

- Something you want your listeners to do: *'I urge you to donate to the RSPCA immediately.'*

- Something you want your listeners to feel: *'We have what it takes to make this our best sales month ever.'*

- Something you want your listeners to think: *'This policy will dramatically improve our profit margins.'*

- Something you want your listeners to remember: *'Our company is the leader in wireless technology.'*

## COMPUTEREASE PRESENTATION TO WIDGET SOLUTIONS

**What action do we want the Widget team to take after the presentation?** We want them to sign up for a trial of our training services.

**How will we ask them to do this?** *'Try our training programme for three months and you'll see results. I guarantee it.'*

**What would you like your audience to do, feel, think or remember after your presentation?**

_____

_____

_____

_____

_____

**How will you ask them to do feel, think or remember it?**

_____

_____

_____

_____

_____

_____

## 7. Say thank you

After you've delivered your core message, supporting arguments and call to action, you're finished your winning presentation. Now you have to find a graceful way to leave the podium or open the floor for questions.

One of the best ways to close is by thanking both the event organisers and the audience. Be genuine, but quick.

There's an added advantage to ending your presentation with a thanks: It's an excellent signal for your listeners to give you a big round of applause!

## How do I give a presentation without sounding like an ad?

In many cases, but especially at industry conferences, your event organiser may tell you, 'We want you to share your expertise, but we don't want this to be an ad for your company.' You, of course, want to make sure your listeners know the benefits of your product or service. How do you accomplish both?

The key is to make sure you help your listeners learn something meaningful, even if they never use your products or services.

One effective way to accomplish this is to keep the bulk of your comments focused on the general topic of your presentation, but use your own products or services when you give specific examples.

For instance, if you work for a publishing company, and you've been asked to speak about technology developments for publishers, you'd devote the majority of your presentation to explaining industry trends and innovations. But when giving examples of how those trends and innovations work in real life, you'd explain how you used them in your new line of *In A Day* books.

Your audience will recognise that you're drawing on your own experience for examples, and they'll listen without feeling like they're hearing a commercial.

## QUICK**TIP**

### What NOT to Say

How do you know what *not* to share with an audience? A few guidelines:

● When speaking outside your own business, don't reveal your company's financial performance. Avoid specific figures. Use percentages instead. Rather than saying sales increased from £1 million to £1.4 million, say that sales increased by 40%. Check your company policy on what you may say. If this information is proprietary, say only that sales increased significantly. Even if an audience presses you for specifics, you are not required to share proprietary information.

● Never reveal company secrets or information that haven't been made public.

● Don't name specific clients unless they have agreed to act as case studies.

● Never discuss personalities. If the biggest problem you faced when launching your new product was that the division manager never made his deadlines, you must not share that in your presentation. While you can be more forthcoming in an internal presentation, be careful not to embarrass or complain about others in a group setting.

## Pulling It All Together: Content

Your content is the centre of your presentation. Many people fret about what to wear or how to stand on stage but pay too little attention to crafting and honing their content.

The key to creating effective content is understanding what you want to say, what your listeners want to hear and what you want them to do when your presentation is over. Being clear about your goals makes it easier to select your content.

And remember, choosing your content is a process of deciding what to leave *out* as much as what to leave *in*. Your job as a presenter is to decide what's important so your audience doesn't have to.

# 3

## Accomplishments

*In this step you'll:*

- ☐ 1. Learn about the building model
- ☐ 2. Construct your presentation opening
- ☐ 3. Organise the body, or pillars, of your presentation and select the subpoints to support your main arguments
- ☐ 4. Draw your conclusions and issue a call to action

## Time-Saving Tools

*You'll complete this step more quickly if you have any of the following handy:*

- ☐ 1. Your core message from Step 2
- ☐ 2. Your call to action from Step 2

# Step 3:
# Organisation

QUICK**TIP**

**The Shape of
Things to Come**

Rather than just being a formless flow of facts and figures, winning presentations have a shape. Your presentation can be constructed like a building, as outlined in this Step. It can be crafted like a newspaper story, with the most important information provided at the beginning and the least important at the end. Or you can use a story framework; setting a scene, adding details, building interest, and rewarding the audience with a conclusion. Whatever shape you choose, clear organisation gives your content a framework that lets you build a solid case for your core message and call to action.

**W**here do you start your presentation? Where do you finish? What do you say in the middle? Once you've figured out *what* you're going to say, you have to figure out *how* to say it.

A solid organisational structure can make the difference between a winning presentation and one that leaves an audience bored or befuddled. It's not enough to have meaningful content; you have to present that content in a manner that is comprehensible—and convincing.

No matter how you choose to organise your presentation, or how much time you have to give it, *all* effective presentations include:

- **An opening.** Gains the attention of your audience, explains why the topic is important to them and introduces your core message

- **A body.** Offers the main arguments that support your core message, convinces your listeners to agree with it and makes them responsive to your call to action

- **A conclusion.** Restates your core message, provides a summation of your key arguments and gives your audience a specific call to action

Or, to put it another way:

- Tell the audience what you're going to tell them

- Tell them

- Tell them what you just told them

# 1. The building model

**BUILDING MODEL OF PRESENTATION STRUCTURE**

When creating your presentation, it helps to visualise something that represents its structure. One proven image is that of a *building*. You can easily fit the content you selected in Step 2 into the framework provided by the building model.

The different parts of your presentation can be represented by the three main parts of a building. It does not have to be a complicated one. Think back to the simple, solid buildings you used to make with blocks as a child.

Like that block building, your presentation will have three basic components:

- **A foundation.** The opening, in which you introduce your core message.

- **Pillars.** Supporting arguments, which hold up your core message and help convince your audience of your point of view.

- **A roof.** The conclusion, in which you review your core message and main arguments and issue a call to action.

In this section, you'll use the building metaphor as a guide for organising your content. Keeping the image of a building in mind reminds you that you've got to do more than just present a list of facts or figures to your listeners. You've also got to shape that information, constructing a strong, solid case for your message from the ground up. Every element of your presentation needs to support and enhance the other portions of your talk.

# 2. Lay your foundation

Hook or Attention-Getter

Opening (Foundation)

The foundation of your presentation is its opening. Your opening sets the tone for the entire presentation. It's during your opening that your audience decides whether to pay attention, whether they'll be receptive to you and whether you have something valuable to say.

Let's face it: Not every member of your audience will listen to absolutely every word of your presentation. Unless you're a truly riveting speaker, or giving a very short talk, at some point listeners will find their minds wandering. After all, audience members, who are used to channel or Web surfing, are no longer accustomed to paying attention for long periods of time.

You've got the best chance of capturing your listeners' full attention at the beginning of your presentation. So make the most of that opportunity.

A strong opening typically contains, in order:

- **A hook or attention-getter.** Effective hooks can be compelling news items, intriguing statistics, amusing or emotional anecdotes, stimulating questions, or any other device that immediately captures the interest of your audience.

- **The reason for your presentation.** Stating this in your opening shows listeners that you understand why you're giving your presentation and what it means to them.

- **Your core message.** This is what you want your audience to remember. You will repeat this core message, perhaps rephrasing it in different ways, a number of times throughout your presentation.

Use the worksheet on page 45 to outline your opening and build the foundation of your presentation.

## COMPUTEREASE PRESENTATION TO WIDGET SOLUTIONS

### Opening

**Hook**

£520,000. That's what Widget Solutions threw away last year on outside, emergency tech support for problems that should have been handled in-house. £520,000 for computer problems that would have been easily resolved by your existing employees, had they been equipped with the proper training. And that doesn't even address the costs of employee down time, the time and money that slipped away as staff waited for someone else to come in and fix their machines.

Strong appeal to budgetary concerns

**Reason for Presentation**

I'm going to show you how, by spending just a fraction of that figure, you can reduce your dependence on outside tech support and save hundreds of thousands of pounds for your company.

Shows value of programme in terms of future savings

**Core Message**

The unique training programme developed and tested by ComputerEase can save Widget money. We will significantly enhance the skill sets of your employees. We can equip them with the knowledge and tools to resolve the basic technical problems that occur on a day-to-day basis. That means Widget saves money and you and your team can get back to work.

Benefits beyond cost savings

**Use this worksheet to construct your opening.**

How will you open your presentation? What type of hook can you use to capture the attention of your audience? (Will you use a news item? An anecdote? A joke? A question?)

_____

_____

_____

_____

_____

_____

_____

Why are you giving this presentation? (Be sure to state the reason from the perspective of your audience, not your perspective.)

_____

_____

_____

_____

_____

_____

What is the core message you want your audience to remember? In what ways will accepting your message benefit your audience?

_____

_____

_____

_____

_____

_____

_____

_____

_____

# 3. Organise the body

The body of your presentation is grounded in the foundation and holds up the roof. A presentation's body is made of the arguments—facts, examples, explanations—that support your core message and lead to your conclusion and call to action.

Main Arguments (Facts, examples, observations)

Each of your arguments, or pillars, should help make the case for your core message. They make you, and your message, more convincing. Ideally, these arguments will be so solid, that your audience can't help but draw the same conclusions as you.

While the body is the most important part of your presentation, it's also the part of your presentation during which your audience are most likely to drift off and begin doodling, staring out the window, or playing with their Blackberries.™ So you have to make certain that each of your major arguments packs a punch.

## Remember the Rule of Three

How many arguments should you use to support your core message? Three. Winning presentations follow the rule of three: three main arguments support the core message and no more than three subpoints (or pieces of evidence) support any main argument.

Your audience can only absorb so much. If you provide too much evidence in support of your message, you'll lose your listeners' attention. Even if you don't, wading through too much information makes it hard for them to decide which facts are the most important. You want them to focus on the three most compelling reasons to agree with your message.

Will limiting yourself to just three main arguments be frustrating? Yes, sometimes. After all, you know a whole lot more than you can squeeze into just three explanations. And you've got way more than three reasons your listeners should agree with you.

The process of selecting your three most compelling arguments will force you to home in on only the strongest evidence in support of your core message rather than throwing a whole shelf-full of explanations and data at your audience. And remember: Your listeners don't need to know *everything* that you do.

## Subpoints

If you want to provide more information, or you have a lot of time for your presentation, you can add subpoints to your three major arguments. As with your major points, these subpoints can be data, examples, or explanations that support the position you make in your main argument. Again, limit yourself to no more than three subpoints to support any main argument.

If you choose to add subpoints, the central body of your presentation would be organised like this:

I. First main argument

    a. Subpoint

    b. Subpoint

    c. Subpoint

II. Second main argument

    a. Subpoint

    b. Subpoint

    c. Subpoint

III. Third main argument

    a. Subpoint

    b. Subpoint

    c. Subpoint

## COMPUTEREASE PRESENTATION TO WIDGET SOLUTIONS

### Body

**Argument 1:** ComputerEase saves you money.

- **Subpoint:** CE training costs only a fraction of what Widget spent on outside tech support. The figure was £520,000 last year, spent on skilled outside IT consultants. We're offering you a special year-round employee training package for £95,000.
- **Subpoint:** On an hourly basis, CE's programme costs less than the county's off-site training programmes. (£65 per hour for CE, as opposed to £85 per hour for local off-site classes.)
- **Subpoint:** Widget will realise even more cost savings through enhanced employee efficiency.

**Argument 2:** ComputerEase enhances your employees' efficiency by 50 per cent.

- **Subpoint:** Proven in tests with client user groups.
- **Subpoint:** Better than sending employees to off-site training programmes. We come to you. (Keeps employees on-site.)
- **Subpoint:** Employees don't waste time waiting around for tech support. They learn how to quickly resolve problems themselves and get back to work.

**Argument 3:** Better-trained staff enhance the productivity and profitability of your company.

- **Subpoint:** Employees can better assist customers, increasing customer loyalty and repeat business.
- **Subpoint:** Employees overcome problems more easily, allowing your company to get on with the business of making money.
- **Subpoint:** Greater employee confidence and higher job satisfaction translates into lower staff turnover and a more stable company.

**What are the main arguments you will make in the body of your presentation? What are the subpoints (evidence, statistics, reports, case studies) that support each main argument (if any)?**

**Argument 1:**

Subpoint 1:

Subpoint 2:

Subpoint 3:

**Argument 2:**

Subpoint 1:

Subpoint 2:

Subpoint 3:

**Argument 3:**

Subpoint 1:

Subpoint 2:

Subpoint 3:

# Alternate Presentation Structures

The building model provides a solid organisational structure for a winning presentation. However, there are other ways to organise your presentation. The way you choose to organise your presentation depends on the purpose of your presentation and the amount of time you have to give it.

A few alternate presentation structures:

**Step-by-step lesson.** For lengthy training sessions, you'll organise your presentation as a step-by-step guide through the information your audience needs to know. Break down the process you're explaining into steps and encourage questions from the audience throughout.

**Storytelling.** A well-told story can provide a compelling illustration of a situation or an important argument while keeping your audience listening to your every word. Storytelling is not appropriate for most business presentations; it's most likely to fit in at a banquet or retreat, when the audience is more relaxed and expects to be entertained.

**Chronological recitation.** Present the history of the events as they occurred rather than focusing on highlights. This is not usually a very powerful structure for a presentation, but it may be the most appropriate when giving background information, such as reporting on how a product was developed.

**Newspaper-style report.** Newspaper stories are written with the critical information in the first paragraph (*who, what, when, how, why*) and subsequent information given in descending order of importance. This way editors can easily lop off stories from the bottom when there's not enough room in the paper. You, too, can top-load your most important information, saving the least important details for the end. This structure is particularly useful when you're not sure how long every member of the audience will stay and you want to make certain they hear the critical details even if they leave before you're finished.

## Rhetorical Devices

Accomplished speakers often use rhetorical devices—
techniques of phrasing or language that add power to their
message—to evoke an emotional response from listeners.
Some effective rhetorical devices:

### Series of Three:

'Friends, Romans, Countrymen…' – *William Shakespeare*

'We can not dedicate, we can not consecrate, we can not
hallow this ground.' – *Abraham Lincoln*

### Contrast:

'Ask not what your country can do for you; ask what you can
do for your country.' – *John F. Kennedy*

'Being sober on a bus is, like, totally different than being
drunk on a bus.' – *Ozzy Osbourne*

### Repetition:

'I have a dream that one day this nation will rise up and live
out the true meaning of its creed.

I have a dream that one day on the red hills of Georgia the
sons of former slaves and the sons of former slave-owners will
be able to sit down together at a table of brotherhood…

I have a dream that one day even the state of Mississippi…
will be transformed into an oasis of freedom and justice.

I have a dream that my four children will one day live in a
nation where they will not be judged by the colour of their
skin but by the content of their character.' – *Martin Luther
King*

QUICK**TIP**

**One Size Fits All**

One advantage to organising
a presentation using the building model is that this makes
it easy to lengthen or shorten
your remarks. If you arrive at
your event and discover that
the organisers have cut your
presentation time from forty
minutes to ten, you won't
need to panic. You can simply
eliminate the subpoints without losing the main thrust of
your presentation.

# 4. Draw your conclusion and give a call to action

**W**hat do you want your audience to remember? What do you want them to do? The last portion of your presentation is often the part your listeners will remember most. But many presenters run out of steam after they've been talking for a while, and their presentations seem to trail off. Be certain you still have enough focus and energy to make a strong finish.

Link back to Opening Attention-Getter

Closing Remarks

Restate Core Message, Call to Action

Your conclusion is the roof of your building; it tops off the structure and brings everything together.

In your concluding remarks you:

- Briefly **review** your main arguments (your pillars)

- Powerfully **restate your core message** (your foundation)

- Give audience members a **call to action**

- **Link** back **to your opening hook** (optional)

- **Thank** the organisers and audience

**Review your main arguments.** First, briefly review the information presented in the body of your presentation. The emphasis here is on *brief*. Your listeners just heard this information; the review is a way for you to bring the body to an end and move to your close, not a summary.

**Restate your core message.** Next, and most importantly, *directly* and *emphatically* restate your core message. You don't want any confusion about the meaning of your presentation. Your message now carries more weight with your audience, since it has been bolstered by the arguments you presented (your pillars). Don't be afraid to tell your audience what you want them to remember: *'My recommendations will cut costs by 30%.'*

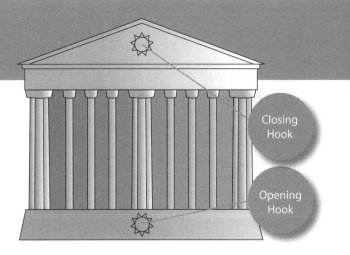

**Present the call to action.** Your closing remarks must point your audience in a particular direction. This is where you tell your listeners what that direction is. As you saw in Step 2 (on page 35), your call to action should be:

- Something you want your listeners to do
- Something you want your listeners to feel
- Something you want your listeners to think
- Something you want your listeners to remember

Don't be afraid to be very specific. This is one of the most important—if not *the* most important—aspects of your presentation, so you need to make sure the audience understands *exactly* what you'd like them to do next.

**Link back to your opening hook.** Some of the most memorable presentations end by looping back to the opening hook that originally captured the listeners' attention. By bringing back your opening device, your presentation comes full circle and gives your audience a sense of completion.

For example, if you were giving a presentation about a diet and exercise programme, you might have opened your talk with an attention-grabbing story about an overweight man named George being rushed to the hospital with chest pains. Your closing comments could bring your audience back to George: *'One year after enrolling in our programme, George is thirty pounds lighter, runs two miles a day and looks forward to many more happy years with his family.'*

**Thank your listeners.** Finally, thank the audience, and the organisers if appropriate, for their time and attention. Keep your thank yous very general and very brief; *'I want to thank Chris for putting this programme together and all of you for coming.'* You want people to leave remembering your core message and call to action, not the names of the people who helped you set up the projector.

Use the worksheet on page 54 to develop the conclusion of your presentation.

## COMPUTEREASE PRESENTATION TO WIDGET SOLUTIONS

### Conclusion

**Review of Core Message and Key Arguments**

As you can see, the benefits you will realise from our services extend far beyond enhancing your employees' skill sets. Like our other clients, you'll see their impact in increased employee and customer satisfaction, a smoother, more efficient workflow and a more stable workplace with less staff turnover. Most importantly, you'll save money—and make more money as well. Try our training programme for three months and you'll see results. We guarantee it.

Summarises motivating factors from opening and body. Presents a call to action.

**Closing Remarks**

What would you do with an extra £520,000? Expand your office space? Buy new equipment? Launch a new marketing campaign? Or maybe just organise a few exciting and productive employee retreats. How you use it is your choice. We'd just like to help you put that money back in your budget to spend as you see fit, while at the same time, improving your company's operations and bottom line. With ComputerEase's Training Services, we can make it happen.

Links back to opening hook. Leaves audience motivated to act. Thanks audience.

---

What is your core message? Restate the message here, reviewing key arguments from the body. If your presentation is intended to persuade or inspire, include a call to action.

_____

_____

_____

_____

What are your closing remarks? What do you want your audience to do after your presentation? (Try to link some part of your closing back to the information or images presented in your opening.)

_____

_____

_____

_____

# Funny Business

Should you open your presentation with a joke? Should you pepper your presentation with amusing stories or comments?

Some of the best presentations—and some of the worst—rely on humour. The difference lies in knowing when and how to use it.

Humour can be an effective tool, enhancing your presentation by:

- Breaking the ice with an audience, relaxing both you and your listeners.

- Making you seem more likeable and therefore more credible.

- Creating a bond between you and your audience, since you're both in on the same joke. Once again, that makes you more likeable and credible.

- Entertaining your audience, increasing the likelihood that they'll pay close attention to you and your message.

But you can easily go wrong when you try to be funny. So be careful to follow these guidelines when using humour:

- **Use relevant humour.** Ideally, try to tie your jokes or amusing comments to your topic.

- **NEVER use off-colour, racist, or sexist jokes**. Remember, you're giving a *business* presentation. In addition to offending many of your listeners, jokes like these are inappropriate and possibly illegal.

- **Use self-deprecating humour.** If you can poke fun at yourself without undermining your sense of authority, it shows your audience you don't take yourself too seriously.

- **Don't get carried away.** An opening joke can break the ice with an audience, but you're not expected to be a comedian. A dash of humour is sufficient for a business presentation.

- **Know your limitations.** If you're not naturally funny, don't try to be funny in your presentation.

# Pulling It All Together: Organisation

Once you've clarified your core message and built a solid framework for it, you're well on your way to a winning presentation. Winning presentations start with substance, not style.

Draw from the information you provided in the earlier worksheets in this step to organise the content of your complete presentation.

## Making the Transitions

To enhance the flow of your presentation and help your audience better navigate through it, you'll need to add short transitional phrases. These appear between the opening and the body of your presentation and then again between the body and the conclusion. If you add subpoints, you may also want to add transitions between them as well.

Don't struggle too hard to come up with great transitions. These don't have to be particularly clever. You'd be surprised by just how well simple phrases such as, *'As you can see…'* or *'Another example of this is…'* or *'In conclusion…'* work.

In a presentation on the need for a new office facility, you might move on from your opening to your body with this statement:

*'Our current facility no longer meets our needs. Here are three reasons why …'*

The transition from the body to the conclusion of your presentation serves as a review of your message and your three main arguments:

*'As you can see, our current facility is inadequate. It was designed to accommodate far fewer people than we now employ, it does not have the power capacity to handle our new computer systems, and it is too far away from our customer base.'*

Good transitions serve to guide your audience through your presentation, helping them (and you) know where you are, making it easier for them to grasp and accept your message.

**Use this worksheet to organise your presentation.**

How will you open your presentation? (See worksheet on page 45.)

_____

_____

_____

_____

_____

_____

_____

What will you include in the body of your presentation? (See worksheet on page 49.)

_____

_____

_____

_____

_____

_____

_____

How will you conclude your presentation? (See worksheet on page 54.)

_____

_____

_____

_____

_____

_____

_____

## COMPUTEREASE PRESENTATION TO WIDGET SOLUTIONS

### Title: FastTrack to Success
### Opening

**Opening Hook**

£520,000. That's what Widget Solutions threw away last year on outside, emergency tech support for problems that should have been handled in-house. £520,000 for computer problems that could have been easily resolved by your existing employees, had they been equipped with the proper training. And that doesn't even address the costs of employee down time, the time and money that slipped away as staff waited for someone else to come in and fix their machines.

**Transition: Reason for Presentation**

I'm going to show you how, by spending just a fraction of that figure, you can reduce your dependence on outside tech support and save hundreds of thousands of pounds for your company.

**Core Message**

Through the unique training programme developed and tested by ComputerEase, we can significantly enhance the skill sets of your employees. We can equip them with the knowledge and tools needed to resolve the basic technical problems that occur on a day-to-day basis. That means Widget saves money and you and your team can get back to work.

### Body

**Transition from opening:** Here are three ways our training programme can benefit Widget Solutions. First:

**ARGUMENT 1**

ComputerEase saves you money.

- **Subpoint:** CE training costs only a fraction of what Widget has spent on outside tech support. As mentioned, the figure was £520,000 last year, spent on skilled outside IT consultants. We're offering you a special year-round employee training package for £95,000.
- **Subpoint:** On an hourly basis, CE's programme costs less than the county's off-site training programmes. (£65 per hour for CE, as opposed to £85 per hour for local off-site classes.)
- **Subpoint:** Widget will realise even more cost savings through enhanced employee efficiency.

**Transition:** Secondly, your productivity will increase.

**ARGUMENT 2**
ComputerEase enhances employees' efficiency by 50 per cent.

- **Subpoint:** Proven in tests with client user groups.
- **Subpoint:** Better than sending employees to off-site training programmes. We come to you. (Keeps employees on-site.)
- **Subpoint:** Employees don't waste time waiting around for tech support. They learn how to quickly resolve problems themselves and get back to work.

**Transition:** Finally, you'll see the impact of our programme in your bottom line.

**ARGUMENT 3**
A better-trained staff enhances the productivity and profitability of your company.

- **Subpoint:** Employees can better assist customers, increasing customer loyalty and repeat business.
- **Subpoint:** Employees overcome problems more easily, allowing your company to get on with the business of making money.
- **Subpoint:** Greater employee confidence and higher job satisfaction translates into lower staff turnover and a more stable company.

**Transition to Closing:** These are just a few of the ways we can help your company. Our current clients have reported many more benefits, such as smoother workflow processes, stronger relationships with strategic partners and an increase in new ideas and product innovations originating from the employees we've trained.

## Conclusion

**Review of Core Message and Key Arguments**
As you can see, the benefits you will realise from our services extend far beyond enhancing your employees' skill sets. Like our other clients, you'll see their impact in increased employee and customer satisfaction, a smoother, more efficient workflow and a more stable workplace with less staff turnover. Most importantly, you'll save money—and make more money as well. Try our training programme for three months and you'll see results. We guarantee it.

Call
to
Action

**Closing Remarks**
What would you do with an extra £520,000? Expand your office space? Buy new equipment? Launch a new marketing campaign? Or maybe just organise a few exciting and productive employee retreats. How you use it is your choice. We'd just like to help you put that money back in your budget to spend as you see fit, while at the same time, improving your company's operations and bottom line. With ComputerEase's Training Services, we can make it happen.

# Aristotle: Father of the Modern Presentation

While public speaking played a role in many early civilisations, historical documents point to ancient Greece and Rome as the places where it truly became an art form. The Greek philosopher Aristotle (384–322 B.C.) discussed the principles of effective public speaking in his book *Rhetoric*. For Aristotle, persuasion centres on three principles:

- *Ethos*. The speaker's credibility

- *Pathos*. The speaker's emotional appeals

- *Logos*. The speaker's logical appeals

Aristotle's principles have survived the test of time, so keep these three principles in mind as you formulate your presentation.

4

## Accomplishments

*In this step you'll:*

- ☐ 1. Learn a more effective speaking style
- ☐ 2. Learn to overcome fear of speaking
- ☐ 3. Learn effective body language
- ☐ 4. Discover how to dress for a successful presentation

## Time-Saving Tools

*You'll complete this step more quickly if you have any of the following handy:*

- ☐ 1. Information about the size of the audience and the room you'll be speaking in
- ☐ 2. Information about how formal your presentation setting is to be

# Step 4:
# Delivering Your Message

It's not just what you say, but how you say it. Whether or not your message will make an impact on your listeners depends on how well you communicate it to your audience: your delivery.

The better you deliver your presentation, the better you'll connect with your listeners, drive home your message and convince your audience to share your point of view.

The quality of your delivery depends on how you speak, gesture, move and dress. Even if you have a fear of public speaking (a fear shared by many celebrities and experienced public speakers), you can learn to keep that anxiety under control.

Occasionally presenters get away with poor delivery skills. But these presenters are often experts in their field or well-known individuals who have established credibility with their audience before they were ever asked to present. Their loyal listeners will go the extra mile to make sense of what they say. But that's the exception, rather than the rule.

Effective delivery techniques will help you forge a stronger connection with your audience and make them more receptive to your message.

QUICK**TIP**

**How Do You Get to the CBI?**

Practise, practise, practise! If you're giving an important presentation, it's a good idea to practise your presentation ahead of time, especially if you're a relatively new presenter. Practise alone first, then either videotape your presentation or ask someone to watch and listen as you demonstrate your delivery techniques. Many professional presenters report that they have to give a speech dozens of times before it feels polished. You don't have to go that far, but practising even a few times will significantly increase your confidence and abilities.

## QUICK**TIP**

**Where Did Your Audience Come From?**

Consider the background of your audience when choosing your words, speed and style. If you're speaking to an audience whose first language is not English, speak clearly and slow down! Remember, many members of your audience will be translating what you say as they listen. That takes more time.

# 1. Speaking style

What makes for good vocal delivery?

- **Volume.** Nothing is more frustrating than not being able to hear a speaker's words. Arrive at your venue early to check out the audio system, get used to the mike and adjust your volume accordingly. Consider the ambient noise in the room, such as clinking dishes if you're speaking at a meal function or noise from an adjoining room at a conference hall, and speak louder to compensate.

- **Clarity.** Pronounce your words clearly. This is particularly critical in two situations: in large rooms and when speaking without a microphone in a room of any size. What you say may be hard to comprehend in a big room, where sound bounces around and your words get muffled or distorted. If you aren't using a mike, your words will be harder for listeners to grasp even when you're in a small room.

- **Speed.** It takes sound longer to travel to the back of a large room than to the back of a small one. Slow down when giving a presentation in front of a big group. When you're nervous, you naturally speed up when talking, so take a breath and reduce your speed.

- **Pacing.** A change of pace attracts attention. Incorporate meaningful pauses to add emphasis in key spots. Slow down when making a vital point, repeating your core message, or giving your audience a call to action.

- **Tone.** Check your pitch. People tend to speak in a slightly higher voice when they're nervous. Try to make certain your tone sounds natural.

- **Authority.** Audiences respond better to speakers who project an air of certainty and confidence. Avoid starting sentences with phrases such as, *'I'm not an expert, but…'* or *'You may not agree with me, but…'* Be careful not to use an upward inflection that makes it sound as if you're asking your audience a question when you're actually making a statement.

## Strong Language?

Strong language makes for strong presentations. Vivid, action-oriented and powerful words bring your presentation to life. Passive and tentative words bore your audience and weaken your authority. As you create your message, review it for weak words and phrases. Use powerful language to strengthen your content and credibility.

| Weak Words | Powerful Words |
|---|---|
| May, Might, Possibly, Should | Will, Do |
| Hope, Believe, Think | Know |
| Try | Accomplish, Achieve |
| Form of the verb 'to be' (is, was, were, am) | Active verbs (succeed, create, save, build, eliminate, win, triumph, beat, overcome) |
| Passive phrasing ('Sales were increased'.) | Active language ('We increased sales'.) |

QUICK**TIP**

**Celebrity
Stage Fright**

Tony Bennett seems to be the epitome of cool, calm and collected. But he suffered from such severe stage fright that he had to soak in a bathtub filled with ice cubes before opening night. Bennett is in good company. Many people in the public eye have struggled with potentially crippling bouts of stage fright, including John Lennon, Stephen Fry, Helen Mirren and Elvis Presley. By learning to control their fears, these celebrities achieved remarkable success. With a little practice and positive thinking, so can you.

# 2. Fear of speaking

It begins about ten minutes before your presentation: your heart starts to pound, your palms sweat, your tummy rumbles. You've got stage fright. Take heart; you're not alone. Public speaking tops most polls as people's greatest fear.

Even the most experienced presenters usually feel a bit of anxiety before they take the stage. A little nervousness can actually be beneficial. It gets your adrenaline flowing, energises you and helps you think more clearly during your presentation.

The key is to make your nerves work *for* you, instead of *against* you. It's OK to have butterflies in your stomach as long as you get those butterflies flying in formation.

You can get your stage fright under control if you:

- **Recognise your valuable role as a presenter.** You're giving this presentation because you have something important to say; you have information the audience wants or needs. Remind yourself that you *belong* at the front of that room.

- **Remember you're there to help others.** Take the focus off your nerves and concentrate on the needs of your audience. You will relax when you stop thinking too much about yourself.

- **Arrive early and talk to members of your audience.** Meeting and speaking to a few of your listeners *before* you get up to give your presentation will help you relax and establish a rapport with them before you begin.

- **Keep in mind that the audience wants you to succeed.** Most people arrive at a presentation expecting the speaker to do reasonably well. Audience members are typically willing to cut a speaker a lot of slack before passing harsh judgments. Listeners are on your side.

- **Write out your opening remarks.** Typically, your nerves subside after you've begun speaking. If you're afraid of a shaky start, writing out your opening section can provide you with an emotional prop. Remember, though, that this technique is just to get you off the ground. It's deadly to *read* a presentation to an audience.

- **Troubleshoot potential problems.** You'll be more at ease if you know your computer will work, the mike's adjusted and there are enough chairs for everyone in the audience. Consult the Troubleshooting section on pages 192–193 for a complete checklist.

- **Practise, practise, practise.** You'll feel much more confident if you are familiar with your content, your PowerPoint slides and the key aspects of your presentation.

- **Think positive.** It may sound trite, but thinking positive, rather than negative thoughts makes you more relaxed. Stop telling yourself, *'I'm going to fail'*, or *'They're going to think I'm an idiot'*. Instead, give yourself positive messages, such as, *'I know my stuff'*, *'These people really need this information'*, and *'I'm going to nail this presentation'*.

- **Visualise your success.** Close your eyes and picture yourself mastering every stage of your presentation, eloquently making each argument and delivering a brilliant conclusion. Do this several times, especially just before the event. Top athletes and performers swear by positive visualisation as an element of success.

## QUICK**TIP**

### Oh, Yeah?

Try to keep your facial expression neutral even when someone says something you think is stupid, gets angry, or disagrees with you. Never frown or scowl when listening to an audience member ask a question or make a comment. It is especially important to avoid any negative facial expressions, however slight, when listening to another member of a panel discussion. If you can't stop yourself from looking annoyed, glance down or make notes. Showing disrespect to the audience or another member of a panel reduces your credibility and likeability.

# 3. Body language

How you use your body—how you stand, sit, move and gesture—affects how an audience receives your message. If your body language communicates confidence, sincerity and enthusiasm, people will be more likely to believe you. If not, they'll have a harder time accepting what you say.

Knowing how to move in front of an audience helps you add emphasis to key points, communicate your message, and overcome physical obstacles between you and the audience (such as poorly placed podiums, mike stands and equipment, or oversized rooms).

Strong body language includes:

**Standing.** When you stand before an audience, your posture should convey strength, steadfastness and power. You want to appear alert, engaged and authoritative.

- Stand up straight; be careful not to slouch, even if you're tired.

- Don't lean on anything, including the podium or table.

- Stand still except when moving intentionally to make a point or connect with a portion of the audience; don't fidget.

**Moving.** Moving occasionally—and deliberately—during your presentation adds visual interest and conveys a sense of energy.

- Move purposefully from one side of the stage to the centre, then to the other side, to connect with your entire audience throughout your presentation, especially if it's fairly long.

- Use movement as punctuation. Stop moving when you're making an important point.

- If the room is set up with a podium, try to move away from it occasionally if the microphone can go with you. If you need the podium to hold your notes or advance your PowerPoint presentation, use it but avoid getting stuck behind it.

- Avoid turning your back on your audience.

- Move toward any audience member you are trying to engage. If you're trying to disengage (as when discouraging more questions), move away.

**Sitting.** You may give a presentation from your seat during a panel discussion, informal interview, or in a workshop. Even when sitting, you want to appear alert, engaged and authoritative:

- Sit up straight or lean slightly forward. Make certain you don't slouch.

- When sitting at a table, keep your hands on top of it, rather than under it.

- When participating in a panel discussion, turn your head toward the speaker whenever other members of the panel are speaking.

- When sitting on a stage, sit with your legs together, feet on the floor or crossed at the ankles. Don't cross your legs.

**Gesturing.** Using gestures adds emphasis to key points, provides visual interest and makes you seem relaxed. But too many gestures can look fidgety, distracting your audience and making you appear less authoritative.

- Adjust the size of your gestures to the size of the room. In a large hall, your audience will be unable to see small gestures. In a small room, big gestures seem silly.

- Vary your gestures often. Using the same one repeatedly can annoy your audience.

- Turn your palms up, rather than down, when gesturing. An open palm is welcoming, inviting new ideas and encouraging responses.

- Use your hands to draw the shape of an object in the air, or to symbolise opposing views, using the right hand for one point, the left for another.

### What Do I Do with My Hands?

Many presenters are stumped by something that seems very simple: what to do with their hands while they speak. When you're not gesturing or using a prop, the best place for your hands is by your sides. You can also rest them on the podium or on top of a table.

Avoid:

- Putting them in your pockets

- Placing them on your hips

- Crossing them in front of your chest

- Playing with a pen, pointer, or prop

- Pointing at anyone

**Eye contact.** One effective way to bond with your listeners is to establish and maintain eye contact as you speak. Eye contact can create the appearance of movement even when you're standing or sitting still. This can be important when you have to remain seated for your presentation or are trapped behind a lectern.

- Look in the direction of a portion of the audience rather than looking directly at one person.

- Shift your gaze from one small section of your audience to another when changing your train of thought or after completing a main argument; maintain eye contact throughout one train of thought or sentence.

- You can give the appearance of eye contact even in a darkened room by looking in different directions at the audience.

- Look at other panel members when they're speaking.

- Looking at one person can make them nervous. Unless you're answering a question, avoid looking at any individual for long.

- Avoid staring at your PowerPoint slides unless pointing out important data.

# 4. Wardrobe

Twenty years ago, it was easy to know what to wear when you gave a presentation: a business suit. But as workplace attire became less formal, wardrobe choices for presentations widened and choosing what to wear for a presentation became more confusing. Making matters more difficult is the fact that many presentations are given in non-business settings, such as a resort, golf course, even Disneyworld.

Since people form their initial opinions within the first few seconds of seeing you, it's important to pay some attention to your wardrobe when planning your presentation.

Factors affecting your choice of wardrobe include:

- **Audience attire.** Dress at or above the level of your audience.

- **Location.** Dress less formally at a resort or casual setting.

- **Type of presentation.** Dress conservatively when giving a major presentation or a sales pitch.

- **Time of day.** Dress more formally for evening events.

- **Day of the week.** You may be able to dress more casually when giving presentations on the weekend.

- **Region.** Some areas, such as Silicon Valley, are more informal than others, such as New York or the City of London.

- **Season.** Make certain your clothes are appropriate for the time of year.

# Ten Tips for Choosing Your Clothing

1. Check with your meeting organiser about appropriate and expected dress.

2. Aim to dress on par with the *best-dressed* person in the room. It's better to be slightly overdressed than underdressed, as it shows respect for your audience.

3. Err on the conservative side, especially in business situations. Dress in business casual only if the situation is clearly informal, such as an off-site business retreat at a ski lodge or golf course. Bring a business suit along anyway, and keep it in your car or hotel room in case you realise upon arrival that others at the event are dressed more formally than expected.

4. Remember, the first word in the term 'business casual' is 'business'.

5. Make sure your clothes fit correctly. Do not wear anything that's too tight or too loose.

6. Avoid anything too glitzy or glamorous unless it's appropriate for your industry or situation.

7. Choose colours that project authority. Select strong neutral colours such as black, gray, or dark blue to be safe. Use strong, bright colours (for women in suits, for men in ties) to project power and keep all eyes focused on you.

8. Make certain your accessories complement, rather than distract from, your wardrobe. Avoid flashy or glittery jewelry.

9. Remove calculators, Blackberries, cell phones and other bulky items from your pockets. Switch the phone off!

10. Check yourself in a mirror before you present. See that there's nothing on your teeth, nothing attached to your shoes or clothing, nothing unfastened or unzipped.

## QUICK**TIP**

### Colour Associations

Some colours have psychological or sociological associations:

- Blue, black and gray are conservative and indicate authority.

- Earth tones suggest home and hearth and are non-confrontational.

- Red signifies power and energy, but sometimes seems confrontational. Red stands for good luck in many Asian cultures.

- Yellow is associated with cheerful, approachable, easy-going attitudes.

- Green often signifies growth or movement and is associated with the environment.

- Purple is often used by those who are in the arts or New Age community.

# Pulling It All Together: Delivering Your Message

A strong delivery style increases your credibility. How you move, stand and gesture all contribute to whether your listeners find you authoritative, knowledgeable and likeable.

When you're a new presenter, it may seem unnatural to pay attention to your speaking style and body language. But working on techniques to improve your delivery skills pays off and increases your audience's ability to grasp your message and respond to your call to action. The better your delivery, the more likely you are to give a winning presentation.

# Notes

5

## Accomplishments

*In this step you'll:*

☐ 1. Learn how to interact with your audience during a presentation

☐ 2. See how room arrangement can affect your presentation

☐ 3. Learn how to manage a question-and-answer session

## Time-Saving Tools

*You'll complete this step more quickly if you have any of the following handy:*

☐ 1. A description of the room you're going to be presenting in

☐ 2. A list of questions you've been asked in the past and the answers you've given

☐ 3. Prepared responses to hostile questions

# Step 5:
# Audience Interaction

**Y**ou're not in this alone. Whenever you give a presentation, you're in the company of a group who can be a vital part of your success—the audience.

Encouraging audience participation breaks down the wall between you and your listeners. By bringing you psychologically—and often physically—closer to your audience, interaction can be a powerful tool for establishing rapport. Making a successful connection with your listeners improves the chances that they'll be receptive to your message and the likelihood that you'll give a winning presentation.

You'll have a number of opportunities to interact with your audience. You can start your presentation by taking a brief poll, or you can solicit comments from your audience during the middle portion of your presentation. You can also take questions from the audience at the end of your presentation.

While you may not want to encourage audience participation at all those opportunities, it's a good idea to set aside some time to interact with the people who are in the room with you. Your listeners will appreciate the chance to ask questions, make comments, or be included in other ways.

QUICK**TIP**

**Before You
Get There...**

If you're presenting to a group of people you don't know, ask your event planner to give you the names and contact information of a few attendees. Call them and find out about their knowledge of your topic and their concerns, and ask them what they hope to learn from you. You'll improve the quality of your presentation and you'll already have a few friends when you walk into the room.

## QUICK**TIP**

### Questions Bring Answers

Asking a few questions at the beginning of your presentation breaks the ice with your listeners and helps you customise your content right from the start. For example, if you were giving a presentation about the growth of the pet products market, you might ask, *'How many of you have pets?'* If several people raise their hands, you could ask them how much they spent on their pets last month. If they spent a lot, you could use their experience to demonstrate the promise of the growing pet market. If, on the other hand, you discover few in your audience have pets, you'll know you're going to have to be even more convincing to make them understand why people spend billions of pounds on their pets every year.

# 1. Interaction during your presentation

Virtually every presentation includes some audience interaction at the end of the talk—it's called the question-and-answer (Q&A) session. But audience interaction doesn't have to wait until you're finished speaking. You can give a more energetic and engaging presentation when you incorporate the audience during the course of the presentation itself.

Some types of presentations, like workshops, demand audience interaction throughout. If you wait until the end before you allow your listeners to ask questions or make comments, they will feel frustrated. During other types of presentations, such as keynote speeches, it's more difficult to solicit audience feedback.

Ways to include the audience during your presentation:

- **Ask for a show of hands.** Take a quick poll about an issue related to your topic. This is a good way to show listeners you're interested in them. And it has the added benefit of helping you shape your content to better relate to the audience's needs.

- **Ask the audience to share personal experiences related to your topic**. Take the microphone out to your audience, Oprah-style. Doing so helps you gather stories to support your message, while getting you closer to your audience. But don't lose control of the mike or you may also lose control of your presentation.

- **Ask for volunteers from the audience.** (Plant some if you doubt that any will come forward.) Call these brave souls to the front of the room to help you demonstrate a product or act out a scenario (in a training programme). When you bring a member of your audience into your space, the rest of the audience feels closer to you, too. It transforms them from *spectators* to *participants* in your presentation.

## 2. Working the room

The arrangement of your meeting space can have a major impact on the success of your presentation. A presentation that's a huge hit when given around a cozy conference table might be a complete flop when the speaker has to stand up on a stage, far from even the first row of listeners.

Call your event organiser well in advance of your presentation to ask about your room. Find out about the size and arrangement of tables and chairs. If possible, request the setup that works best for your presentation. If you're the only presenter, and you've arrived early, don't be afraid to rearrange the room to better suit you.

In many cases, though, especially at large conferences or conventions or when you appear on a panel, you'll be stuck with whatever setup already exists. If you can't move tables or chairs, you can often reposition yourself to be closer to the audience when you speak. Even if you don't plan on interacting with listeners, it's a challenge to connect with your audience when there's lots of space between you.

### Think Globally

When giving a presentation internationally, familiarise yourself with the behavioural and cultural norms of the country you're in and adjust your programme accordingly. What might be a hit in Tooting could prove disastrous in Sydney.

Consider these issues when presenting globally:

- Use examples, statistics and quotes from the country in which you're presenting.
- Be especially careful when using humour. Jokes rarely travel well.
- People in some countries are hesitant to ask—or answer—questions. Ask your event organiser how receptive your audience is likely to be to audience interaction before including it in your presentation.

For more information on international communications norms, go to:
**www.international-business-etiquette.com.**

## QUICK**TIP**

### Take Them Away

If your room is set up for many more people than you expect, remove extra chairs before attendees arrive. It's much harder to connect with listeners when there are lots of empty seats.

## Classroom Setting

This design usually allows for maximum visibility. If the room is set up with large aisles and plenty of space between the chairs or tables, you'll have an easier time interacting with the audience. Angle the tables on each side so they form a 'V'. This increases your visibility and creates even more aisle space.

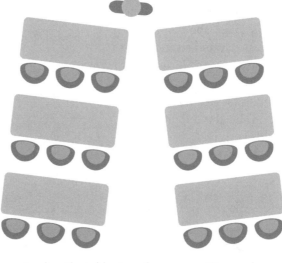

*Angling the tables in a classroom setting makes viewing and interaction easier.*

## Horseshoe Shape

If your room contains long tables, and your audience is relatively small, consider a horseshoe setup. This arrangement makes it easier for participants to interact with each other, which may be important in a policy or strategy session. It also provides maximum visibility for you, the speaker, and gives you easy access to every participant.

## Small Corporate Conference Room

Corporate meeting rooms are intimate environments designed for twenty people or fewer and are best for decision-making meetings. Most boardrooms have rectangular or oval tables, making it fairly easy for everyone to interact with you and each other.

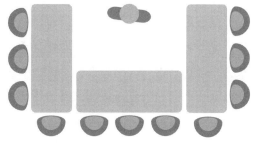

*The horseshoe-style setup provides for optimal interaction.*

*A conference-table setup encourages participation from all.*

## Large Conference or Convention Venue or Banquet Room

Interaction can be challenging in a large room. You're usually high up on the stage, perhaps behind a podium, with the audience fairly far away. In this situation:

- Request an arrangement that encourages more interaction.

- If that's not possible, see if the podium can be removed and use a mike.

- If the setup cannot be changed, do the best you can to move out from behind the podium. The audience will appreciate your attempts to reach out to them, in spite of the obstacles.

- Ask meeting planners to provide a moderator who can solicit questions from the audience.

- Be sure to use large gestures. Unless there's a big video screen above the stage projecting an up-close image of you, most people won't be able to see your face.

- If possible, move toward the front of the audience to engage participants in the front row. Be sure to repeat what they say to the rest of your audience.

*Long, rectangular meeting rooms with podiums make interaction more challenging.*

# 3. The question-and-answer session

Most presentations include some time for questions from the audience. Your event organiser should tell you how much time to set aside for Q&A, but even if you're giving a relatively brief presentation, leave time at the end for a few questions. It shows listeners you're there to meet their needs.

Q&As are designed to help your audience more fully understand your message and arguments. But they also offer many benefits to you as a presenter:

- They allow you to demonstrate your expertise on the topic.

- They provide another opportunity to interact and build rapport with the audience.

- They help you gauge whether an audience understands and accepts your message.

- They provide feedback that helps you strengthen your presentation the next time you deliver it.

Q&A sessions can have a downside:

- You may be asked questions you can't answer.

- They can give a platform to someone who wants to discredit your message or undermine your authority.

- A member of the audience may make a long, rambling statement rather than ask a question.

- Since Q&As usually come last, they can close your presentation on a flat or sour note.

You must finish your presentation—completely and powerfully—before you take questions. When you know you're going to be opening up the floor to questions, it's easy to let the prepared portion of your remarks trail off: '*Um…I guess that's it unless anyone has any questions.*' Since you want your listeners to focus on your core message and call to action rather than on the Q&A session, you have to create a verbal break between the two.

Only after you come to your conclusion and thank the organisers and the audience (and wait for the applause to subside), should you inform your audience that you'll take their questions.

Let them know how much time to expect for Q&A rather than leaving the impression that time is unlimited. You can say: '*We now have time for a few questions*'. That makes it easier for you to cut off questions when you need to.

When someone asks you a question, follow this three-step process.

1. **Listen carefully and attentively to the question** and repeat it for all to hear. Unless the room is very small, never assume that everyone can hear the entire question.

2. **Pause and think about how best to answer the question.** Allow yourself a few seconds to construct a response. This increases the chance that you'll give a good answer. The audience will easily accept a short pause before you plunge into a response.

3. **Answer the question as directly as possible.** Be concise if time is an issue; expand on your answer if you have time to fill. Think carefully; consider the best response.

After your answer, quickly move on to the next question. Avoid asking any questioner whether you answered their question adequately. Although it may seem like a polite gesture, it usually gives that person an invitation to ask another question or to say something that undermines your credibility, such as *'Well, not really…'*

*The three-stage Q&A process*

# Troubleshooting Your Q&A Session

**Keep Your Cool**

In the face of hostility, remain calm. Avoid arguments *at all costs*. Instead, try to identify the underlying concern of the hostile individual and address it in as non-confrontational a manner as possible. Acknowledge that you understand the questioner's concern, even if you don't agree with it. Then use your well-prepared responses and backup data to diffuse the hostility. Even if you are unable to satisfy your attacker, you're likely to win the support and respect of your audience.

**Problem: You don't know the answer to a question.**

**Response:** Resist the temptation to wing it or, worse, to pretend that you know the answer. You risk giving the wrong answer and it's possible someone in the audience knows the correct one. Instead, give the questioner your contact information (which should be on your handouts), and ask her to email the question to you so you can look up the information.

**Problem: The question is unrelated to your topic.**

**Response:** Try to be as helpful as possible, but explain that the question isn't really within your area of expertise. Chances are that other audience members will also recognise that the question is unrelated.

**Problem: The answer to a question is proprietary and confidential.**

**Response:** Try to answer the question in general terms, rather than giving away specifics. If pushed, explain to the audience that you're not able to share the information. Your listeners will respect your need to protect privileged material.

**Problem: Your listener doesn't ask a question, but rather, tells a story or gives a long explanation of a problem.**

**Response:** As soon as there's even the slightest pause, ask the listener if they have a question, or thank them for their comment and move on to the next questioner. Use body language, like backing away, to subtly indicate that their time is up. If absolutely necessary, politely interrupt.

**Problem: No one asks a question.**

**Response:** This makes you feel as if you have not connected with your listeners. In reality, most people are just too shy to be the first to raise their hand. Try to get the ball rolling with a sample question of your own: *'One thing many people have asked me in the past is…'*

Another approach is to plant a trusted colleague or friend in the audience with a question. This takes away listeners' fear of being first and provides you with the opportunity to answer a softball question.

**Problem: You receive a hostile question.**

**Response:** It's not likely that you're going to change your listener's mind. Instead, you want to limit the negative impact that the hostile question will have on the rest of the audience.

First, rephrase the question in terms that are more favorable to you. You can even agree with some aspect of what was said to take the wind out of the questioner's sails. Then use the hostile question as a springboard for giving a positive message.

Here's an example of a hostile question directed at a hypothetical speaker raising money for a charity's teen volunteer programme, along with an appropriate response:

**Question:** *How can you be so naive as to think teenagers will have anything to do with a programme like yours? Aren't we better off spending our money on programmes with a greater likelihood of success?*

**Response:** *You're asking me what it is about our programme that will appeal to teenagers. Let me explain. First, I, too, was sceptical that teenagers would be interested in volunteering, but market research shows that teenagers will volunteer for organisations like ours if they believe in the cause. Second, we provide perks, like free tickets to movies and concerts, to kids who sign up their friends. Finally, as I said earlier, we've already seen a huge increase in teen volunteers—from 1000 to 5000 this year alone. With your help, we can expand our programme to reach even more of these great kids.*

## QUICK**TIP**

### After Your Presentation

You've got one last opportunity to interact with your listeners after your presentation concludes. As some audience members are drifting out of the room, others may approach you with specific questions or concerns. Make certain you don't allow one person to monopolise you.

When possible, mingle with people before they depart. This helps them leave with positive feelings about you.

You or your presentation organiser can also ask attendees to fill out a brief evaluation. Don't be afraid of negative feedback, which you're more likely to get on paper than in person. Learning what didn't work with an audience helps you improve your presentation and you'll be better prepared the next time.

## 4. Conclude your Q&A

Many presenters spend hours honing their high-impact openings and closings, only to end their Q&A session with a whimper. How often have you heard: *'Well, there are no more questions? So, thanks for coming.'*

Your message and call to action, should be the last words your audience hears. Be sure to restate these at the end of your session. Here's how the fictional speaker on page 87 might conclude:

*'Those were all great questions. I've enjoyed speaking with you this evening and showing you how our programme can successfully get teens off the street and involved in rebuilding their communities. Thanks in advance for your support, which is critical to helping us expand this innovative and life-altering programme. Good night.'*

Use the worksheet on pages 90–91 to outline your Q&A troubleshooting plan and create a high-impact ending to your Q&A session.

## COMPUTEREASE PRESENTATION TO WIDGET SOLUTIONS

### Q&A

**No-Questions Response:**

Other clients have asked about our off-site centres. While we prefer to do training on your premises for your employees' convenience, we do offer training sessions on evenings and Saturdays at our Cosmo Street training facility. If you're considering that option for any of your departments, I have brochures here with more information on that programme.

**Potential Hostile Question:**

**Question:** You may charge less per hour than Keystone Skills Centre, but I've heard your programmes are not as comprehensive. People don't learn as well with you.

**Response:** Keystone is well established in this area and definitely has a high-quality programme. However, we've compared standard industry certification scores of 120 people who attended Keystone's programme and 120 who experienced ours. Our students on average performed 50 per cent better than Keystone's students. And 98 per cent of our students went on to receive their certification after completing the appropriate course, compared to 87 per cent of Keystone's students.

**Q&A Closing:**

I've enjoyed talking with you today and explaining how our programme can save you hundreds of thousands of pounds, while strengthening the skills of your employees and improving your company's efficiency. We're eager to start working with you on a three-month trial basis, in which time you will certainly begin to see the results. Here is our brochure and contract. I'll be in touch later this week to see what you've decided. In the meantime, please call me with any additional questions on how we can help mitigate your IT concerns. I enjoyed meeting you all.

How will you conduct your Q & A session? (Simple questions? Index Cards? Moderator?)

_____

_____

_____

What will you do if no one asks questions? (Plant someone in the audience? Ask sample questions yourself?)

_____

_____

_____

Consider possible questions, including hostile questions. How will you respond?

Question 1:

_____

_____

_____

_____

Response:

_____

_____

_____

_____

Question 2:

_____

_____

_____

_____

Response:

_____

_____

_____

_____

Question 3:

Response:

Write your Q&A closing:

# Pulling It All Together: Audience Interaction

Want to keep your audience members awake and alert? Interact with them at every stage of your presentation. By calling on your listeners to make comments, ask questions, or respond to your enquiries, you can keep them involved and engaged every minute you're up in front of them.

It helps, of course, to make certain that your room is arranged so that it's easy for you to move around and interact with audience members. Talk with your event organiser in advance so you can get the room setup that works best for you.

With practice, you can learn techniques for fielding questions, handling problem questioners and deftly ending your Q&A session so that you leave your audience impressed, remembering your core message, and determined to respond to your call to action.

## Accomplishments

*In this step you'll:*

☐ 1. Learn how to work effectively with speakers' aids, including:

- Notes
- Microphones
- LCD projectors

☐ 2. Learn to work with low-tech visual aids, including:

- Flipcharts and whiteboards
- Handouts
- Transparencies
- 35mm slides and projectors
- Props
- Video and audio equipment

## Time-Saving Tools

*You'll complete this step more quickly if you have any of the following handy:*

☐ 1. A list of the speakers' aids you plan to use
☐ 2. A list of the low-tech aids you plan to use

# Step 6:
# Working with Visual Aids

**A**udiences—and presenters—cannot live by PowerPoint alone. It may be difficult for some PowerPoint-dependent presenters to imagine, but plenty of effective presentations were delivered before the advent of presentation software. Take Abraham Lincoln's Gettysburg address, Winston Churchill's 'Never Surrender' speech, or Martin Luther King's 'I Have a Dream' speech, to name just a few. None of these needed PowerPoint slides to make a major impact.

Your visual aids, whether you're using handouts, whiteboards, or videos, should always be chosen and designed to reinforce your core message and lead your audience to your call to action. Remember, it's just as easy to distract your listeners with low-tech visual aids as it is with high-tech ones.

## QUICK**TIP**

### Hello, My Name Is...

Ask your event organiser to give audience members name tags or name plates (if sitting around a table). You'll find that these are an essential visual aid for you, the speaker, especially when speaking to a small group, including audience interaction in your presentation, or running a training programme or workshop.

# 1. Speakers' aids

## Notes

The most important visual aid you'll use is one that is meant to help you, not the audience. These are the notes you'll prepare to help you remember what to say and when to say it.

Whether you use note cards, full sheets of paper, PowerPoint notes, or the back of your hand, the key things to consider are whether:

- You're comfortable using these notes, or you can get comfortable using them.

- You can read them in the room where you'll be giving your presentation; there's enough light to see your written notes or the room is dim enough to see your computer.

- You can maintain eye contact with your listeners as you use your notes. An occasional glance at your notes is all you'll need to guide you.

- Your notes are effective in prompting you on what to say next. They give you enough information to keep your presentation on track.

The most popular options for speakers' notes are:

**Note cards.** The most effective way of using 3"×5" or 5"×7" note cards is to include a few key words or phrases—not complete sentences—on each card to serve as a reminder of where you are in your presentation and what you want to say.

The advantages of note cards are many:

- You can easily rearrange, remove, and even add cards up to the very last minute.

- They are relatively non-obtrusive. Small cards can fit into the palm of your hand; audiences are used to seeing presenters with note cards, even if the presenter is moving around the room.

- Most importantly, you're more likely to merely glance at note cards as you make your presentation; it's tempting to *read* from sheets of paper.

**The entire presentation written out word by word.** Writing out your presentation in its entirety has advantages: it helps you think through exactly what you want to say and gives you more time to choose your words or phrases. But, except in rare instances, writing out each word of your presentation is a way to help you *prepare* for it, rather than a way to create the finished product you present to your audience.

*Reading* your speech from sheets of paper is a recipe for disaster. It's deadly for the audience and they're likely to wonder why you didn't just pass out the written version for them to read on their own.

There are two narrow exceptions to this rule, however. It's OK to read a speech word for word when you're using a teleprompter. And if you're a highly experienced speaker who has already memorised your speech, you'll be able to give it while glancing only occasionally at the text. Realistically, however, few presenters use teleprompters or are experienced enough to read from a written speech without boring their audience to tears.

**PowerPoint slides.** Your PowerPoint slides are meant to reinforce your message, not be your complete presentation. Far too many presenters depend on their slides as a script for their remarks. They then spend the entire presentation looking at the slides rather than connecting with their listeners.

## PowerPoint Notes

PowerPoint includes a feature that enables you to create **Notes** for each slide. (See page 138.) This feature allows you to see any notes you've made on your own computer while your audience sees only the presentation slide on the screen.

Once again, however, using notes makes it tempting to glue your eyes to your own computer screen rather than make eye contact with your listeners.

One alternative is to print out the **Notes** page from PowerPoint (to do this, switch to the **Notes Page** view in PowerPoint) and keep them with you during your presentation. Having your notes on hand prevents you from being glued to your computer screen and is a safer bet if you're unsure where you'll be standing in relation to your computer.

## Microphones

Any time you're speaking to more than a handful of people, it's wise to use a microphone. If listeners have to strain to hear you, it's easy for them to get distracted. As a rule of thumb, if you're speaking to more than fifteen people, request a mike.

As a presenter, you may encounter a number of different types of microphones. It's OK to ask for the type you prefer.

**Radio microphone (lapel or pendant mike).** In most cases, a radio mike that is attached to you or your clothing is the microphone of choice. It lets you move around and keeps your hands free. The lapel mike has three components: a very small capsule (the actual microphone), which clips to your clothing or goes around your neck, a small transmitter/volume control box that attaches to your clothing and a thin wire that connects the two.

Typically, you'll clip the mike to your lapel, the transmitter to your waistband, and run the wire beneath your jacket or blouse. If you know you're going to be using a lapel mike, wear clothing that will allow you to use it. There is nowhere to attach a lapel mike or transmitter on a sheath dress.

**Hand-held microphone.** A hand-held mike is the best choice for presentations that include audience interaction. Like lapel mikes, hand-held mikes (especially cordless hand-held mikes), make it easy for you to move around, but have the added advantage of being easier to use when asking for questions or comments from the audience. However, you must hold the mike throughout your presentation and sometimes deal with a cord. If you're using note cards, too, this can be particularly awkward.

Practise with a hand-held mike before your presentation to achieve a comfortable sound volume. And when asking an audience member to speak into the mike, hold on to it. Once someone else gets their hands on the mike, it may be hard to get it back!

**Lectern with microphone.** Many presenters enjoy having the refuge of a lectern. Lecterns draw the attention of the audience, give you a place to rest your notes (and a glass of water) and provide an emotional haven.

Lecterns, however, create a barrier between you and your listeners and prevent you from moving around to add emphasis, point out something on a slide, or interact with your audience. It's difficult to give a lively presentation from behind a lectern, so avoid them when possible.

**Standing microphone.** You may occasionally encounter a microphone on a floor stand. Sometimes this may be a hand-held mike placed in a stand. If it is, you'll be able to keep your hands free by leaving the mike in the stand. You'll also be able to lift it out and interact with the audience when you choose. However, a microphone fixed in a stand creates the same barrier between you and the audience as a lectern. Avoid using them, if possible.

## QUICK**TIP**

### Laser Pointers

Laser pointers are new alternatives to old-fashioned metal or wooden pointers. They beam out a small dot of laser light that enables a presenter to highlight features on a chart, graph, or other visuals.

If you have detailed information that you want to draw to the attention of your audience, a laser pointer may be useful. This is particularly true when referring to specific elements on a photograph or map. In other cases, using a laser pointer may actually be distracting, especially if the information is already obvious to your audience.

Keep in mind that laser pointers can pose a risk to eyesight if used incorrectly. Aim them only at inanimate objects (never at people or animals) and keep them away from children. Avoid pointing them at mirrors or reflective surfaces, as the beam could bounce back into someone's eye.

## LCD Projectors

Most PowerPoint presentations will be projected on a screen or large monitor. Generally, you will not be responsible for providing an LCD (liquid crystal display) projector; your event organiser will have one available for use.

If you're bringing your own laptop to a presentation, you shouldn't encounter any problems with compatibility. Virtually all LCD projectors work with virtually all laptops. A simple monitor cable connects your laptop and the projector. (Be sure to bring it with you or confirm that one will be available.)

When using an LCD projector, your responsibilities are to:

- Confirm with your event organiser that there will be an LCD monitor and monitor cable available for you.

- Determine whether you are to use your own laptop or to bring (or email) a copy of your presentation to be shown on the event organiser's computer. If you use an Apple Macintosh laptop then you'll need the adapter that came with it to connect it to a standard projection cable – your host is highly unlikely to have one.

- Ask for, or bring, an extension cord to give you more flexibility in room setup.

- Ensure that you are able to stand where you can both interact with your audience and advance your PowerPoint slides as needed.

- Be sure the projector doesn't cut off anyone's view.

# 2. Low-tech visual aids

In a world full of flashy multimedia, low-tech visuals can provide a refreshing change of pace. You can use them in situations where you don't have access to a computer, or even electricity. Moreover, with low-tech aids, you never have to worry about computer glitches, missing extension cords, or other technical problems.

Low-tech visuals, such as whiteboards, flipcharts and handouts, encourage audience interaction and participation. They are particularly well suited for small groups, planning sessions and workshops. Of course, you can also use them in conjunction with your PowerPoint or other media presentation.

## Flipcharts and Whiteboards

**Flipcharts** are oversized pads of paper, usually placed on an easel. You write on these with permanent or semi-permanent markers.

**Whiteboards** are solid surfaces generally attached to the wall. You write on these with markers and can erase them much as you would a chalkboard.

The advantage of using a whiteboard (rather than a flipchart) is that you generally have a larger space on which to write. The advantage of using a flipchart (rather than a whiteboard) is that you are creating an un-erasable record of your session.

When presenting to groups of more than twenty-five, it may be difficult for all members of the audience to see what's being written on the board or chart.

Remember, an audience faces the same challenges trying to decipher a cluttered flipchart or whiteboard as they would a too-busy PowerPoint slide. And if you spend too much time writing on a whiteboard or flipchart, you won't be able to communicate effectively with your audience. A few other keys to success with these low-tech tools:

- **Write legibly.** Everyone in the audience must be able to read what you have written. Avoid small or skinny letters. Print rather than using cursive script.

- **Stand to one side.** Remember, your audience can't see through you. As soon as you finish writing, move to one side of your chart or board so that all members of the audience can see what's been written.

- **Prepare flipcharts in advance.** If you have a lot of information to discuss, you may want to prepare some pages of your flipchart in advance of your presentation.

- **Write notes to yourself.** In one corner of the whiteboard or using light pencil on the pages of the flipchart, write notes to remind yourself of what you want to or need to cover.

- **Consider attaching flipchart pages to the wall as you complete them.** Keeping notes visible to your audience is helpful, especially when discussing a workflow process, future plans, or a complicated concept. To affix your pages to a wall, use tape or, better yet, purchase Post-It® flipchart pads, which stick to walls without tape.

- **Use marker colours that can be easily seen.** Black and blue markers are the most easily read, especially from a distance, so use these for the majority of your text.

- **Bring spare markers.** It can be disastrous to run out of ink in the middle of your presentation.

## Handouts

Audiences *love* handouts. Presenters aren't always as enthusiastic. Handouts are just one more thing to prepare, and it can be difficult to know how much information to include and how much to save for the presentation. They can also distract your listeners from what you have to say.

In some cases, you'll be required to distribute handouts before your presentation begins. They may contain information your audience needs to be able to participate in a meeting, or be forms you want them to complete as you deliver a workshop or seminar.

In other situations you'll be able to choose whether or not to distribute handouts and when to do it. Should you?

**The pros:**

- **Listeners may pay more attention to your spoken remarks.** If audience members have already received the data you're discussing, or know they'll be receiving it at the conclusion of your presentation, they won't be distracted by taking notes while you're speaking.

- **Listeners can be better prepared.** If you send handouts to participants before your presentation, it's possible that they will arrive better prepared and able to participate in the discussion.

- **You can distribute detailed data.** It's difficult for audience members to get a good look at graphs, charts and data on a screen. If you have detailed information to share with your audience, handouts are a must.

- **Your listeners will better remember you and your message.** When you distribute a handout, your listeners get a physical reminder of your presentation. They also get your contact information so they can reach you in the future. Handouts are an excellent idea when giving a sales presentation.

**The cons:**

- **Listeners may pay _less_ attention to your spoken remarks.** Your audience might flip through the pages of your handout rather than listening to you.

- **Your handouts can spill the beans.** If your handouts contain copies of your PowerPoint slides or other information you want to reveal gradually over the course of your presentation, your listeners may have already skipped ahead. This can make it harder for you to build the case for your core message.

- **Your listeners can leave early.** If you're in a situation where members of your audience can easily leave (such as in a convention hall), some members of the audience may feel as if they can go once they've received your handouts.

Once you've decided _whether_ to distribute handouts, you need to decide _what_ to include on them.

For handouts you're going to pass around at the beginning of your presentation, include:

- Data your audience needs to understand your presentation

- Complicated charts or graphs that would be hard for audience members to see on screen

- Product or service information sheets

For handouts you're going to pass around at the end of your presentation, include:

- Notes from your presentation so listeners do not have to make their own notes while you speak

- Copies of your PowerPoint slides

- Your contact information—an absolute must!

# Handout Hints

At the beginning of your presentation, tell your audience there's no need to take detailed notes. You're more likely to keep listeners' attention if they know that they'll receive handouts with everything they need to remember at the end of the presentation.

Deliver on your promise; pass out nicely designed handouts with detailed notes after you finish. If possible, include more than just copies of slides in your handout. Give your audience a comprehensive outline or explanation of your material, along with plenty of contact information and resources where they can learn more.

Negotiate with your event organisers. When you present at a large conference, event organisers often require you to send your presentation (including copies of your PowerPoint slides) in advance for them to include in conference materials. It may be difficult to get around this practice. If appropriate, request that the organisers distribute your handouts at the end of your presentation to avoid the problem of having audience members skip ahead while you are speaking.

For small groups and planning sessions, send data out ahead of time. If you want to distribute information to participants before your presentation, try to send it out at least two days in advance. That gives them time to review the contents before they arrive, rather than during your presentation.

## Transparencies

Transparencies (also called 'overheads') are old technology. In most business situations, they've now been replaced by PowerPoint presentations.

However, since many offices still have transparency projectors around, and it's so easy to carry transparencies with you, they can work well as a backup for your computer presentation.

Transparencies are also relatively easy to create. In many cases, you can make them by printing your material directly on transparency pages straight from your printer.

You can also handwrite or draw your own transparencies or add notes to them as you interact with your audience during your presentation.

## 35mm Slides and Projectors

Slides and slide projectors are not cutting-edge technology, but they still have some users, especially among photographers and artists, who argue that slides present more vibrant colours and images.

Well-designed slides can add impact to your presentation. If you are using them:

- **Darken the room.** Slide quality diminishes dramatically in a brightly lit or sunlit room.

- **Number your slides in case they fall out of order.**

- **Don't hurry through your slides.** Make sure your audience has a minimum of twenty seconds to view and understand each slide.

- If possible, **bring your own carousel** and run through your slides beforehand to make sure none are missing or upside down.

### Transparency Tips

**Make your overheads readable.** Place your transparency on the floor and look down at it. If you can read the words, they should also be legible to your audience. But if your handwriting is difficult to decipher, don't write on your transparencies.

**Use reveals.** These are strips of paper covering type that you pull away to reveal information a little at a time, rather than all at once.

## Props

A cleverly chosen prop helps your audience remember key ideas in your presentation. It can also add entertainment value. Just make certain your prop reinforces your message and doesn't come off as too gimmicky.

Props can come in all forms, from a piece of equipment that you're demonstrating, to your own product, to an attention-getting device that you can relate to your message. Because few presenters use props, they add another level of interest to your presentation.

When using props:

- **Make sure your prop is clearly visible.** Choose props that are large enough for every member of the audience to see clearly. Objects smaller than your hand can't be seen beyond the first row.

- **Interact with the audience.** Can you find a way for audience members to use your props? For instance, if you're going to be offering a number of reasons why your product can't be compared to your competitor's, you might bring along a basket of apples and a basket of oranges and throw one or the other to members of the audience as you list each reason. (Just make sure you've got a good aim!)

- **Give a prop to everyone.** If you're using a small prop (especially if it's something fun), you may want to bring enough of them for each member of the audience to use (and keep). That way your prop becomes a marketing item.

- **Make sure your prop is visible to your audience**, but doesn't obstruct you or your other presentation visuals. Newspapers, for example, can be used to tie your topic to current events, but avoid holding them in front of your face.

- **Hold onto your prop.** Avoid passing it around, as it will distract your audience. If you want to give them props as well, pass these out before your presentation; give your audience time to examine or play with them, then move on.

- **Make sure your prop works** and you know how to use it. This is especially true with magic tricks, electrical equipment and other props that require setup. Your best bet: avoid those kinds of props unless you've mastered their operation.

- **Use props in moderation.** Once you've made your point with your prop, let it go. And avoid using too many props. They can get old fast and detract from your message.

## Video and Audio Equipment

A good audio or video clip can enliven a presentation, providing a nice change of pace from a speaker standing in front of the room. A video clip can wake up an audience and get them to pay closer attention to your subsequent remarks.

Audio can be used as background sound to enhance PowerPoint slides or other visual displays. Used without any visual accompaniment, however, audio clips can be problematic. What will your audience look at while you play the audio?

Of course, in some business situations, audio by itself may be perfectly appropriate—in the music industry, for instance, or when playing a sample radio commercial for an upcoming advertising campaign.

One way to use audio or video clips is to include them as part of your PowerPoint presentation file (see Step 9). This assumes, of course, that you have the clips in digital form.

However, unless you're a PowerPoint expert, you're generally better off sticking with separate audio or video equipment for your sound or video display. Here's why:

- **Technical issues.** You increase the likelihood of technical glitches when you're dependent on connections between your computer and other systems.

- **Performance issues.** It can be a challenge for a computer to serve out thirty frames per second of high resolution video. The way computers handle that task is to compress the data. The result is that the video can stutter, the picture and audio can get out of sync, or in some cases not play at all.

- **Loss of quality.** At this time, the quality of video and audio is likely to be higher when shown on dedicated audio or video equipment than through PowerPoint on your computer.

*Never* assume that your event venue will have the equipment you need. If you are planning on using separate audio or video equipment, check—and double check—with your event organiser that they'll have both the equipment you need and the correct format for that equipment. This is particularly true if you're presenting internationally.

# Presenting from Afar

By using the telephone or Internet, you can conduct meetings, conferences, training programmes and planning sessions without the time and expense of bringing all the participants together.

- **Internet conferences** (Web conferences, webinars, online training and so on) take place entirely over the Web (using Voice Over IP technology for audio) or combine Internet visuals with telephone conferencing.

- **Telephone conferences** (conference calls) bring a number of people together on the same phone call (typically using conference calling capabilities). PowerPoint presentations or other documents may be sent to participants in advance of the call.

Giving a presentation to people who aren't in the same room with you presents special challenges. The biggest is that participants are easily distracted. When they are sitting in front of their own computers, they can simultaneously answer email, write reports, and check sports scores.

There's also the possibility of a technical snafu, making it difficult for you to present or for some participants to fully engage in the meeting.

Recognise these issues as you plan your presentation and take appropriate steps:

- **Get detailed instructions on using the technology and uploading your visuals (PowerPoint, text) in advance.** If this is your first time using the equipment, try it out before the actual conference.

- **Invite audience participation and interaction.** Ask more questions or invite more remarks from your listeners than you would if you were all in the same room

- **When including a PowerPoint presentation, try to use Internet conferencing software that enables you to control how the slides are advanced.** That way you keep your audience's attention on the points you're discussing. If you send out your PowerPoint presentation to participants in advance, they can easily skip ahead while you speak.

- **Pronounce your words clearly.** Remember your listeners can't see you and may experience uneven sound quality, so they may have a harder time understanding you than if you were in the same room.

- **Keep it short.** Because it's easy to lose listeners' attention online or on the phone, plan your presentation in advance and keep the conversation focused.

QUICK**TIP**

**AV Tips**

A few other tips for using video or audio equipment:

- Arrive at your venue early to try out the equipment and make sure everything works—and works well together. Don't rely on the assurances of the AV crew—test it yourself.

- Bring an extension cord and a multiway plug adapter, just in case.

- If you're using audio or video tape, have your tape cued up in advance to exactly where you intend to play it. That way you won't have to fast forward in front of your audience to find your place.

- Check the sound quality in advance. Older audio speakers can muffle or distort sound to the point where you may decide you're better off eliminating the clip.

## Pulling It All Together: Working with Visual Aids

Both high-tech and low-tech visual aids can work wonders in capturing and keeping your audience's attention. They help listeners remember your core message and stay focused on your presentation. Just remember, regardless of the quality or type of visual aid you use, you must concentrate on enhancing your message. Use moderation; don't overwhelm your audience—or your message—with too many extras. When used correctly, audio and visual aids enhance your presentation, boost your credibility and strengthen your message.

## Accomplishments

*In this step you'll:*

☐ 1. Learn PowerPoint basics

☐ 2. Learn to view and navigate PowerPoint

☐ 3. Learn to use PowerPoint **Notes** during your presentation


## Time-Saving Tools

*You'll complete this step more quickly if you have any of the following handy:*

☐ 1. The title and content for your presentation

# Step 7:
# Getting Started
# with PowerPoint

*Note: These instructions assume you are using a PowerPoint version from Office XP, Office 2003, or PowerPoint 2002 or later. If you have an earlier version of PowerPoint, some of the features described here may not be available.*

If you're giving a business presentation, you're almost certain to use Microsoft PowerPoint® software. Over the last decade, PowerPoint has emerged as the standard business presentation programme worldwide. It's estimated that as many as thirty million PowerPoint presentations are given each day.

There are a number of reasons for PowerPoint's growing popularity:

- **Most businesses use Microsoft Office® programmes**, which usually include PowerPoint, so they already own the programme.

- **It's relatively easy.** If you can use Microsoft Word®, you can use PowerPoint.

- **It's fast**. You can pull together professional looking presentations quickly.

- **It includes a number of templates** to help you put together your presentation.

- **You can add colour and graphics to your presentation easily**, without having to hire a graphic designer.

- **It can be fun.** PowerPoint gives you a chance to dabble in design and experiment with your creativity.

But, as plenty of presenters, and even more audiences, will tell you, PowerPoint has a downside. Most of the criticisms revolve around misuse or overuse of the programme. A few common complaints:

- **PowerPoint presenters focus on form over content.** PowerPoint makes it easy to include lots of information, so presenters forget to clarify their message or organise their content.

- **PowerPoint presentations use more bullets than a cheap Western**. The programme is set up for easy insertion of bullet points. This can result in a tedious presentation and lack of focus on a central message.

- **PowerPoint presenters fail to communicate with their audience.** Many presenters use their PowerPoint slides as notes and spend their presentation looking at them, rather than at the audience.

- **PowerPoint presenters overuse animation, sounds, and special effects.** In many cases, these features have no relation to the message and serve only as distractions.

In this step you'll learn PowerPoint basics. By the end of this section, you should be able to put together your own PowerPoint presentation. In Step 9, you'll learn how to add even greater impact to your PowerPoint presentation.

# 1. PowerPoint basics

The first thing you need to do to get started with PowerPoint is to open the programme:

1. Go to your **Start Menu**

2. Select **All Programmes**

3. Select **Microsoft Office**

4. Select **Microsoft Office PowerPoint**

The *first time* you launch the programme, you'll see a pull-down menu titled **Getting Started** in the upper right-hand corner. (This right-hand task pane changes functions as you work on your presentation, so after you close and re-open PowerPoint, the title of the right-hand task pane may change.)

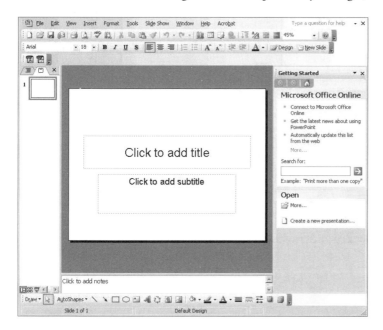

Click the **Getting Started** menu and hold it down to reveal a variety of options.

● Select **New Presentation**. This window appears:

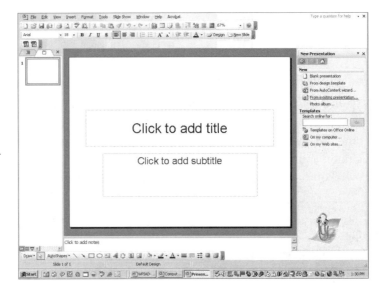

Look at the options under **New Presentation**. If you have not yet developed a presentation, choose either:

● **Blank presentation**, a blank slate where you can enter your content from scratch and then choose your background (see page 120); or

● **From AutoContent wizard**, offering a complete presentation outline that you can customise with your own content and design (see page 126).

# Entering and Enhancing Text

You'll find it easiest to enter and make changes to your text when working with slides in the **Normal** view.

**To add or make changes to the text on a slide:**

1. In the **View** pulldown menu on the top toolbar, select **Normal** view.

2. On the slide in the centre window of the **Normal View**, you'll see text boxes surrounded by dotted lines. Click within the dotted lines where you want to add or change text.

3. Type the text you want to add, or delete text as desired.

**To enhance the appearance of text:**

- Highlight the text you want to change and format it the same way you would in Microsoft Word using the **Format** menu or **Formatting** toolbars to choose font, text size and colour.

To change the number or arrangement of text boxes on a slide:

- Click on the desired **Slide Layout** from the **Slide Layout** task pane in the right-hand column. (See 'Changing the Format of a Slide' on page 119.)

QUICK**TIP**

**Hiding and Retrieving Task Panes in Normal View**

You can increase the workspace/size of the slide you're working on in **Normal** view by closing the right or left task panes. To close a task pane, simply click the **x** at the top of that task pane as you would for any pane in a Microsoft programme.

To retrieve the right-hand task pane, click the **New Slide** button (to get the **Slide Layout** task pane) or the **Design** button (to get the **Slide Design** task pane) in the upper menu bar.

To retrieve the **Outline/Slides** pane (left-hand task pane), go to **View** in the menu bar and select **Normal (Restore Panes)**.

# Moving and Re-Sizing Text Boxes

PowerPoint's design and layout templates automatically position text boxes on your slides.

To change the size of text boxes:

1. Place the pointer over one of the small circles (or squares) at the corners and sides of the text box. These are called the **sizing handles.**

2. When the pointer becomes a **two-headed arrow**, click, hold and drag a **sizing handle** to make the text box larger or smaller.

To change the position of a text box:

1. Place the pointer at any place on the outline of the text box.

2. When the pointer becomes a **four-headed arrow**, click and hold the four-headed arrow and drag the text box to the desired position.

ComputerEase

# Adding and Deleting Slides

You have several options for adding slides:

- Click the **New Slide** button on the upper right-hand side of the formatting toolbar menu; or

- Press **Control M** on your keyboard; or

- In the left-hand column (when the **Slides** tab is selected in the left-hand task pane), click the thumbnail of the slide that appears before the place you want to add a slide and press the **Return/Enter** key on your keyboard. A new thumbnail will appear in both the left-hand column and the centre window.

Among the options to delete a slide:

- In the left-hand column (**Slides** pane), click the thumbnail of the slide you want to delete and press **Delete** on your keyboard; or

- Click the thumbnail of the slide you want to eliminate and, under the **Edit** menu in your toolbar, select **Delete Slide**.

# Changing the Format of a Slide

You'll find that you will want to use a number of different slide formats in your presentation including title slides, slides containing bullet points and slides where type appears with graphics. To change the format of the slide simply:

1. Open a new slide in the centre window.

2. In the right-hand column (the **Slide layout** pane), click on your desired format. The slide automatically changes to that format in the centre window.

You can then add text or graphics as the new format permits.

## Working with a Blank Presentation

One way to develop your presentation is by working with a **Blank Presentation**. To do so:

1. After opening PowerPoint, either go to the **Getting Started** menu and select **New Presentation** or go to the **File** pulldown menu in the upper left of the standard toolbar and select **New**.

2. From the **New Presentation** menu, select **Blank Presentation**. You will see a blank slide in the task pane on the left, a large blank slide template in the centre and a number of options for slide layouts in the task pane on the right.

You can choose any one of the options to the right to begin designing each slide.

Alternatively, you can simply click inside one of the dotted boxes in the slide in the large centre window to add your text and other content.

Use your mouse/cursor to move between boxes and add text, as in this slide:

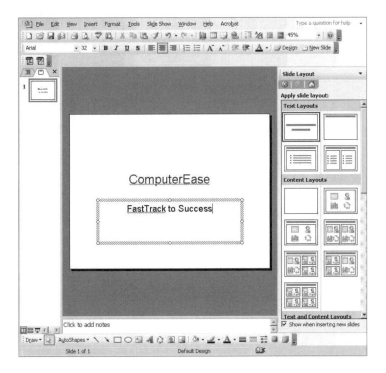

## Adding Colour and/or Design Background to Your Slide

Once you have entered the text for your presentation, you may want to add a design or colour to the background of your slides. The two easiest ways to do this are to choose either a **Slide Design** or a **Colour Scheme**.

To choose a slide design:

1. Open the pulldown menu for the right-hand task pane.

2. Choose **Slide Design**. You will be shown a number of standard slide design templates.

3. Click on the design template that appeals to you. PowerPoint will automatically apply that design to all your slides. (Or, you can right click on a design and choose either **Apply to All Slides** or **Apply to Selected Slides**.)

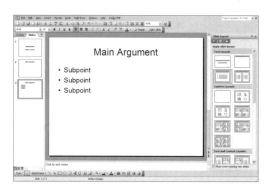

*Slide before design added.*

*Slide after design added.*

To select a plain colour background for your slides or to change the colour once you have selected a design template:

1. From the pulldown menu in the right-hand task pane, which is probably displaying the words **Slide Design**, choose **Colour Schemes**.

2. Click on the colour scheme that appeals to you. PowerPoint will automatically apply that scheme to all your slides. (Or, you can right click a colour scheme and choose either **Apply to All Slides** or **Apply to Selected Slides**.)

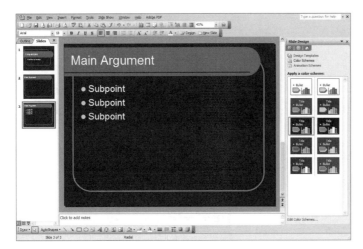

*Slide with colour added*

# Working with Design Templates

Design templates enable you to quickly customise your presentation with a pre-selected design and colour scheme.

1. After opening PowerPoint, go to the **Getting Started** menu and select **New Presentation**.

2. From the **New Presentation** menu, select **From design template**.

You will see the **Slide Design** menu on the right, with a variety of template options listed below the words **Apply a design template**.

When you find a template you like, right click on it and choose **Apply to All Slides.** The design and colour scheme will appear on the slide in the centre, in the **Outline/Slides** pane on the left and to all new slides as you add them.

If you're not fully satisfied with the colour selection on your slide, click **Colour Schemes** in the right-hand task pane. You can change the background colour of your slide without losing the design. You can also experiment with different colour combinations for your titles and bullets.

You'll learn more about working with design templates in Step 9.

### Note

All subsequent slides you create will use this template, unless you right-click on the template and instead choose **Apply to Selected Slides**. You can also choose to change your design template later, just by going back and selecting a new design template and right clicking **Apply to All Slides**.

## Using the AutoContent Wizard

The AutoContent Wizard includes outlines for different types of presentations and provides a quick and simple way to organise your material. You'll find the Wizard particularly useful if you need help figuring out how to organise your content or aren't sure of what type of information to include in your specific type of presentation.

- Under the **New Presentation** menu, click **From AutoContent wizard**. The AutoContent Wizard dialogue box appears:

● After reviewing the overview on the left-hand side of the screen, click **Next >** to bring up this box:

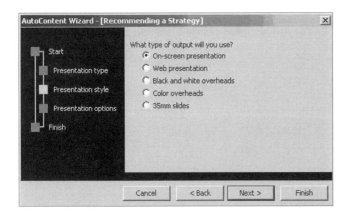

Now:

1. Click each of the category buttons in the centre to view the presentation types in the right window.

2. Click and highlight the presentation type that best describes the one you plan to give.

3. Click **Next >**. This box appears:

Select the visual output type you will be using. Typically, you'll be giving an **On-screen presentation.** Click **Next >**. This box appears:

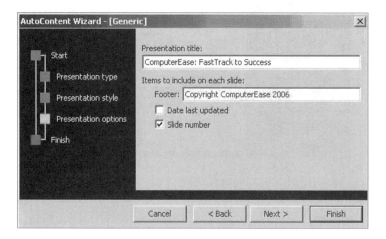

In this box:

1. Enter the title of your presentation in the space allowed.

2. Add any information you'd like to appear on every slide, such as your name, the name of your company, or a copyright notice.

3. Click on **Date last updated** and **Slide number** if you want those to appear.

A template with your presentation title and the other information you entered (along with the name the PowerPoint software is registered to) will then appear on the first slide of your presentation:

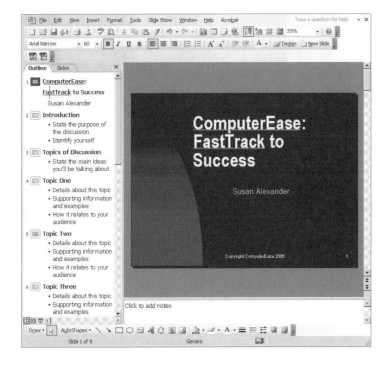

An outline will appear in the left-hand column (the **Outline** pane) suggesting the type of content to appear on each slide according to the presentation type you selected when you set up the AutoContent Wizard.

The outline prompts you to enter your own information in each slide. To do so:

1. Click on a slide/topic in the left-hand column, which then opens that slide in the centre of your screen.

2. In the centre window/slide, click on the text you want to change.

3. Enter your text, moving from one part of the slide to another with your mouse/cursor.

4. Add or delete slides as desired. (See page 119 for instructions on adding and deleting slides.)

To change the background of your slides, click the **Design** button on the formatting toolbar above the right-hand task pane.

This opens the list of **Design Template** options for your **Slide Design**. Click on the design that appeals to you to change the background for your entire slide presentation. (Note that, when you click **Design**, the left-hand column changes from the **Outline** tab view to the **Slides** tab view.)

*Slide with existing design.*

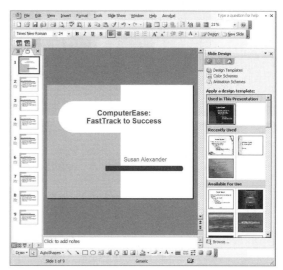

*Slide after design changed.*

## 2. Viewing and navigating PowerPoint

Under the **View** menu at the top of your screen, you'll find many ways to look at, and work with, your PowerPoint presentation. The three most commonly used views:

● Normal

● Slide Sorter

● Slide Show

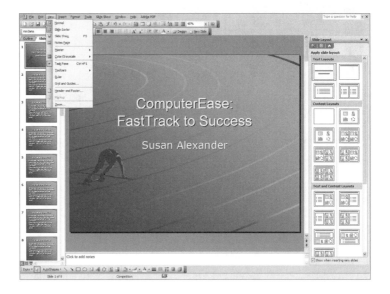

## Normal View

So far in this step, you've worked in the **Normal** view. This is the view in which PowerPoint opens new presentations.

Use the **Normal** view to enter your text and change fonts and type sizes (see page 117). You can also use it to choose your slide layout, design, colours, transitions and add animation. The **Normal** view becomes the default view for working on your presentation.

The **Normal** view shows:

- The current slide in the centre window. You can type your content here.

- A left-hand column which toggles between **Outline** or **Slides** view, making it easy to move from slide to slide, enter or delete slides, or view an outline of your presentation.

- A task pane in the right-hand column which is typically used for opening a new presentation, choosing your **Slide Layout**, **Slide Design**, **Colour Schemes**, **Slide Transitions** (see page 166), or **Animation Schemes** (see page 162).

- A **Notes** pane below the centre window to enter words and phrases to help you in your presentation.

To change the look of your slide—its layout, design, colours, or animation—use the right-hand task pane, using the pull-down menu to navigate between the different choices.

## Slide Sorter

The **Slide Sorter** view offers an easy and useful way to get an overview of your presentation, re-order, or delete slides. You'll find you use it often, especially as you become more familiar with PowerPoint.

The **Slide Sorter** view enables you to see all your slides at once. In this mode, the thumbnail views of all your slides are larger than they are when you're in **Normal** view. This lets you see how the material flows together.

You can easily move slides around in the **Slide Sorter** view; in fact, this is the easiest way to re-order slides.

To move a slide in **Slide Sorter** view simply:

1. Left click on and hold the slide you want to move

2. Drag it to the desired position

3. Release

The slides you've displaced will automatically move to the next position in the presentation.

It's also easy to delete a slide in Slide Sorter view. Simply right click on the slide and select **Delete Slide**. Or, left click on a slide and hit the **Delete** button on your keyboard.

If you want to change text on a slide, simply double click on that slide in **Slide Sorter** view and it will change to **Normal** view for editing.

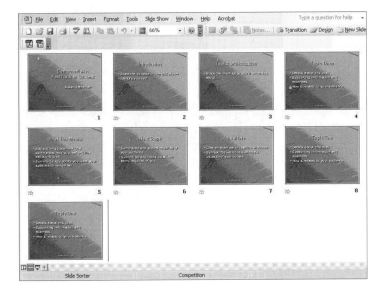

## Slide Show

It's time for your presentation! You'll use the **Slide Show** view to share your presentation with your audience. But you can also use **Slide Show** view to preview the presentation while you're working on it.

To start your presentation from the beginning:

● From the **View** menu, select **Slide Show**: Your presentation will fill the screen, starting from your *first slide*.

There will be times, however, when you want to switch to **Slide Show** mode at points other than the beginning of your presentation. This could happen when you want to see how a slide will look while you're working on your presentation or when you want to select a single slide to look at.

To switch to **Slide Show** mode from any slide:

1. In either **Normal** or **Slide Sorter** view, click on the slide where you want the **Slide Show** view to begin.

2. Click on the small icon that resembles a 'Screen' 🖥 in the lower left-hand corner or click **Shift +F5**.

Your presentation will then shift to **Slide Show** mode starting with the slide you selected.

## Advancing Slides

Once you are in **Slide Show** view there are several ways to advance the slides, including:

- Clicking on them; or

- Pressing the forward arrow key on your keyboard; or

- Clicking the forward arrow in the lower left-hand corner of the slide. (This is one of four very faint small icons you'll see there. The others move your slides forward or backward or provide a way for you to write on your slide.)

Click the back arrow in the slide's bottom left corner (or use the back arrow key on your keyboard) to view previous slides. Clicking the square menu icon in the bottom left corner, or right clicking anywhere on the slide, offers a number of additional options, including:

- Jumping to a specific slide; or

- Choosing a marker or highlighter to make notations on a slide during the show; or

- Inserting a white or black screen (to project when you're speaking and don't want the audience to focus on a slide).

To get out of **Slide Show** mode, you have a number of options, including:

- Pressing the **Escape** key on your keyboard. That returns you to the view you were in prior to switching to **Slide Show** view; or

- Pressing the **Hyphen** key; or

- Right clicking your mouse and selecting **End Show**; or

- Clicking on the square menu icon in the lower left-hand corner.

# Using Notes During Your Presentation

You may want to keep some notes handy to prompt your comments on each slide while giving your presentation. PowerPoint has a way to make this easy.

In the **Normal** slide view, PowerPoint provides a **Notes** pane in the centre window, below the slide.

Enter the comments you want to remember when viewing that slide in the **Notes** area.

When it's time to give your presentation, and you want to view your notes but you don't want your audience to see them, set up your slide show in **Presenter View**.

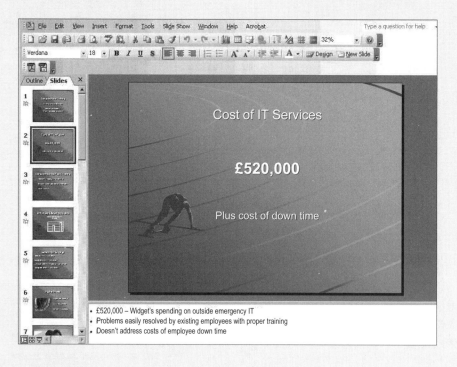

## Setting Up Presenter View

Say you want to view your presentation notes and easily access other controls, while your audience sees only your presentation slides in **Slide Show** mode. You can do this with **Presenter View**, a feature of later versions of PowerPoint.

**Note:** *Your computer must be able to support multiple monitors to enable this feature; in many situations, this means an overhead monitor for the audience and the monitor on your computer for you.*

To set up **Presenter View:**

1. From the **Slide Show** *menu* (*not* the **Slide Show** selection in the **View** menu) select **Set Up Show**.

2. A popup box—**Set Up Show**—will appear. Under **Multiple monitors**, select the **Show Presenter View** check box. (**Note:** Make certain both monitors are connected and on.)

3. In the **Display slide show on:** list, click the monitor on which you want the slide show presentation to appear.

QUICK**TIP**

**Presenter Pointers**

For more information on using **Presenter View**, go to the Microsoft Office website at *www.Office.Microsoft.com*. In the **Search** pull-down menu, select **Assistance**. Enter 'Presenter View' in the search box and click **Go**. When you see the search list, click on 'Presenter view: tools for running a PowerPoint presentation'. It should be the first entry.

## Handy Keyboard Shortcuts

Creating a presentation
(in **Normal** mode):

- Help: **F1**
- Insert New Slide: **Control M**
- Show or remove task pane:
  **Control F1**
- Go to Slide Show: **F5**

Running a presentation
(in **Slide Show** mode):

- Go to the next slide, or perform
  the next animation, any one of:
  - **ENTER**
  - **SPACEBAR**
  - **PAGE DOWN key**
  - **RIGHT ARROW key**
  - **DOWN ARROW key**
  - **The letter N key, or**
  - **Click the mouse**
- Go to the previous slide,
  or perform the previous
  animation, any one of:
  - **BACKSPACE**
  - **PAGE UP key**
  - **LEFT ARROW key**
  - **UP ARROW key, or**
  - **The letter P key**
- Go to a specific slide number:
  Type the **slide number,** then
  press **Enter**
- Display a black screen, or
  return a presentation from the
  black screen:
  - **The letter B, or**
  - **The full stop key**
- Display a white screen, or
  return from a white screen:
  - **The letter W, or**
  - **The comma key**

# Pulling It All Together: Getting Started with Power Point

If you're giving business presentations, sooner or later, you're going to use Microsoft PowerPoint. Audiences have become accustomed to seeing PowerPoint slides and it's far and away the most used presentation software. PowerPoint is an efficient way to communicate, and it's become the standard for business presentations.

Fortunately, it's also fairly easy to use. While PowerPoint is a powerful programme, you can learn the fundamentals quickly. And it's probably already on your computer. Even if you've never used PowerPoint before, you'll be able to put together a basic PowerPoint presentation in far less than a day!

## Accomplishments

*In this step you'll:*

☐ 1. Learn about slide design and content selection

☐ 2. Learn to make effective colour choices

☐ 3. Learn how to use your slides most effectively during your presentation

## Time-Saving Tools

*You'll complete this step more quickly if you have any of the following handy:*

☐ 1. A draft version of your PowerPoint presentation

☐ 2. A diagram of the room you'll be presenting in

# Step 8:
# Slide Rules

The two most important things to remember when designing a PowerPoint presentation are: *Message* and *Moderation.*

**Message.** What you have to say—not how you put it on PowerPoint slides—is the most important part of your presentation. Just because PowerPoint makes it easy to put text on slides doesn't mean that you should just start typing. Make certain you have thought through your core message and the supporting information that will effectively persuade, move and motivate your audience.

**Moderation.** Don't go overboard with PowerPoint features. PowerPoint makes it easy for you to add polish and a little pizzazz to your message. But be judicious in your use of special effects and other PowerPoint elements. Use as few slides as possible to support the verbal part of your presentation and keep them simple. There's no need to show off with snappy special effects, especially if they distract, rather than inform, your audience.

Your slides should complement your verbal presentation— not repeat every word or add distracting information. Resist the temptation to include PowerPoint slides for every point or aspect of your presentation. Give your audience time to *listen* to you, not just read your slides.

# 1. Design and content

It's easy to create attractive, effective PowerPoint slides. Nevertheless, many PowerPoint presenters use poorly designed, hard-to-read slides. No one likes to spend half an hour squinting at tiny text crammed onto a low-contrast background.

Remember: The key to a successful PowerPoint presentation is to create slides that *reinforce* your message, not ones that *repeat* it.

## ComputerEase Training

- ◆ ComputerEase saves you money.
- ◆ CE costs only a fraction of what Widget spent on outside tech support last year.
- ◆ Widget spent £520,000 on skilled outside IT consultants.
- ◆ ComputerEase offers a special year-round employee training package for £95,000.
- ◆ CE's programme costs less than the county's off-site training programmes. (£65 per hour for CE, as opposed to £85 per hour for local off-site classes.
- ◆ Widget will realise even more cost savings through enhanced employee efficiency.

*Ineffective slide: Most audiences would find this slide difficult to read and understand because it contains too much text.*

## The Four-by-Four Rule

The Four-by-Four Rule is simple: Limit the content of each of your slides to no more than four bullet points containing no more than four words each.

Audience members cannot absorb hundreds of printed words and listen to you at the same time. Once you have entered your text on a PowerPoint slide, go back and edit, edit, edit.

Create slides with the goal of using as little text as possible.

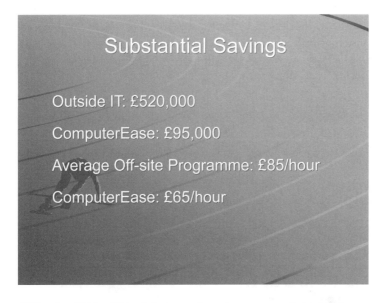

**Effective Slide:** *This slide is much easier to grasp. It highlights the key points the speaker wants to make. Each of these points now has greater impact on the audience.*

## Meaningful Titles

The title on each slide should clearly summarise not just the content, but also the *purpose* of the slide. This is particularly important when showing charts and other representations of numerical data. In the best case, the title conveys to your audience what you want them to *think*.

For example, fictional ComputerEase presenter Susan Alexander wants to highlight a study showing the effectiveness of her company's training programme. She plans to use a chart showing the results of the study. Rather than titling her slide 'Training Programme Study', her title gives the conclusion of the study: 'Enhances Efficiency by 50%'. (Since her whole presentation is about the training programme, there's no need to put 'Training' in the headline here.) The meaning of the chart is right there in the headline.

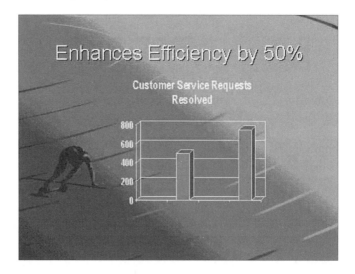

*The title of this slide helps Susan's audience immediately understand the significance of her chart.*

## Type Fonts and Sizes

The key consideration when choosing type fonts and sizes is: What can your audience read most easily?

Choose the largest type size that fits the amount of text you have on a slide. (This is another reason to limit the amount of text on a slide; the less text you have, the larger and more readable your type can be.)

The type size you choose will depend on the amount of text you have on a slide, your background and even the size of room (use larger type sizes for bigger rooms). As a general guideline, however, use the following rules of thumb for font sizes:

- Opening presentation titles: 54 to 80 point

- Slide titles: 44 to 66 point

- Bulleted material: 28 to 40 point

In most cases your audience will find your slides easier to read if you choose a clean, uncluttered typeface. Typically, this means selecting a sans serif font (type without the little 'feet' and flourishes. Arial is probably the most commonly used sans serif font.

It's safest to stick with one font for all your slides. If you do want to vary the look of your slides, limit yourself to no more than two different fonts (one for titles, the other for bulleted points). However, you can still use italics to add additional interest.

| Serif Fonts |
| :---: |
| Garamond |
| Times New Roman |
| Palatino |

| Sans Serif Fonts |
| :---: |
| Univers Bold |
| Verdana |
| **Arial Black** |

## Varying Text and Images

As you become more capable with PowerPoint, you'll want to add to the visual appeal of your presentation by inserting graphics and other images. In Step 9, you'll learn how to use graphics in your presentation.

As you develop your content, be on the lookout for information and graphics to add. Some types of images that work well in PowerPoint:

- Simple graphs or charts

- Photos

- Maps

- Line drawings

The key is that all images should be *simple.* They must be clearly visible to and easily understood by all members of the audience. Many presenters include charts or graphs with rows and rows of data that are incomprehensible to everyone except the people sitting in the first row. Few things are more frustrating to a listener than hearing a presenter discuss details of a graph that can't be seen.

## 2. Colour choices

### QUICK**TIP**

**Colour Challenges**

One thing to keep in mind when choosing colours for a PowerPoint presentation is that some in your audience may be colourblind. The most common form of colourblindness leaves viewers unable to distinguish green from red. This means they won't be able to decipher red text on a green background. Avoid red text in any case, as it's difficult to read on a screen.

In a PowerPoint presentation, colour is more than an aesthetic decision; the colours you choose can make the difference between whether an audience can read your slides or not. Make certain that your text is clearly legible, whether in a brightly or dimly lit room, or from near or far away.

You may want to choose colours that reflect your corporate identity. Perhaps you want the background colour of your slide to be the dominant colour in your company's logo. But if your company's colours make the text difficult to read or do not look good when projected, choose other colours.

If your company's colours were dark red and dark blue, it would be difficult to tell one from the other if they were projected on screen as text and background. Instead, choose one for your background colour and use a contrasting colour (such as white) for your text. Keep in mind that if you are going to include lots of slides or graphics in your presentation, a very dark background (either red or blue) might make them impossible to see.

PowerPoint includes a number of design templates with fairly neutral backgrounds and suggested colour schemes. These are safe choices for most presentations. To learn how to select a **Slide Design**, see pages 122–123.

Limit your slides to four colours at most (not including colour photos): one or two colours for the background and one or two colours for text. Whatever colours you choose, keep your colour scheme consistent throughout your presentation.

## QUICK**TIP**

### Colour Significance

Certain colours have specific associations (see p.72). You may want to keep these in mind as you choose the colours for your presentation:

- **Red:** power, energy, danger; associated with good luck in the Asian community

- **Green:** growth, movement, healing; associated with the environmental movement

- **Blue:** stability, calm, security, business; associated with water-related images

- **Yellow:** cheerful, uplifting

- **Purple:** associated with spiritual meanings for some viewers

## High Contrast

Your slides will be much easier to read if there's contrast between the colour of your text and the colour of your background.

It's usually best if you place light-coloured text (such as white) on a dark background, especially if you'll be projecting your slides in a darkened room. The one exception to this is if you are going to be presenting in a very well-lit or sunlit room. In that case it's better to stick with dark text on a light background.

You can add additional readability to your text, especially light text on a dark background, by making it **bold**. However, make certain you are consistent in your use of bolding throughout your presentation or the text on some slides will look slightly faded.

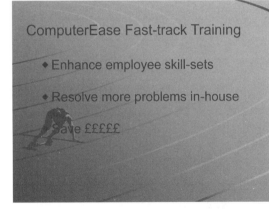

**Low Contrast:** *Dark text on a medium-to-dark background will be difficult for most viewers to read.*

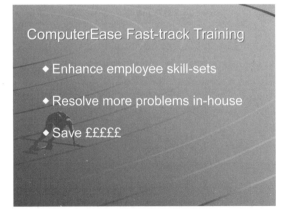

**High Contrast:** *Text colours that contrast with the background are easier to read.*

## 3. During the presentation

QUICK**TIP**

**Getting to the Point**

In most cases, you will *not* want to point to your slides. Remember, *you* are the focus of your presentation, not your slides. However, in some cases, especially when referring to a chart or photograph, you may want to indicate elements on a slide. You can point to the slide as you would to a painting if you were a tour guide at a museum, or you can use a laser pointer.

The impact of your PowerPoint presentation will also be affected by what you do during the show—where you stand, how you refer to your slides and the extent to which you depend on them during your spoken presentation.

## You and the Screen

Be aware of where you are located in relation to the screen. Stand to one side of your slide, not in front of it. It's easy to drift in front of the slides when speaking.

Be careful, however, that you don't end up in complete darkness while your slides are projected. Arrive early enough at your event to make certain that there's enough light to keep the attention focused on you while you're speaking and that you can still be seen while your slides are being projected without having to stand in front of the screen.

## Advancing the Slides

In many cases, you will have to stand close to your computer to control the slides. This will limit where and how much you can move around the room.

In many situations, you'll find there's only a short cable between your computer and the LCD projector, making the room setup, and your location, awkward. You may have to stand to a far side of the room or immediately in front of the screen. This type of logistical detail can hurt your presentation before it even begins.

If possible, bring a remote control so you can advance your slides without having to stay behind your computer. If you don't have a remote control, and the room setup is very awkward, ask someone else to sit at your computer and advance the slides when you tell them to.

No matter what, arrive at your destination early and check out the room to see if you can arrange it so you can easily advance your slides and still be seen by the audience.

## Slide Dependence

A final note: PowerPoint slides are there for the audience—not for you. Your slides are not meant to be your notes.

Look at your PowerPoint slides only to point out specific information, such as data within a graph or chart. You can glance at a slide occasionally to help you keep your place in your presentation, but *never* read your slides; nothing puts audiences to sleep faster than a presenter reading from PowerPoint slides.

Presenters who keep their eyes glued to their slides lose the opportunity to communicate with the audience. Maintain eye contact with your listeners. Stay focused on them and they will stay focused on you.

QUICK**TIP**

**Save the Last Slide**

You want your final slide to be memorable—after all, it's the last thing your audience will see. Moreover, it often stays on the screen during your question-and-answer period. Perhaps the best things to put on your final slide are your name, company name and contact information, especially if you are speaking to an audience outside of your own company. Otherwise, you may want to create a final slide that reinforces your core message.

## Pulling It All Together: Slide Rules

PowerPoint can be a great addition to your presentation, or it can be a great distraction. The key to effective PowerPoint use is knowing how to design and use slides effectively. Don't get carried away: limit both the number of slides you use and the amount of information you put on any one slide. Create a more stimulating presentation by adding photographs, charts, graphs, or other visual images as variation to your text. Make certain there is sufficient colour contrast between the text and background. And remember, the important part is to focus on your message.

# STEP 9: Enhancing Your PowerPoint Presentation

## Accomplishments

*In this step you'll:*

☐ 1. Learn to set up a PowerPoint presentation and create a title slide

☐ 2. Learn to create text animation

☐ 3. Learn to animate bullet points

☐ 4. Learn to add charts and graphics

☐ 5. Learn to combine photos with text

☐ 6. Learn to use unaccompanied photos to reinforce themes

☐ 7. Learn to insert audio files

☐ 8. Learn to create image animations

☐ 9. Learn to create a final slide

## Time-Saving Tools

*You'll complete this step more quickly if you have any of the following handy:*

☐ 1. The first version of your PowerPoint presentation

☐ 2. Any image files you plan to include in your presentation

☐ 3. Any audio files you plan to include in your presentation

# Step 9:
## Enhancing Your PowerPoint Presentation: Advanced Techniques

One of the best ways to learn advanced PowerPoint techniques is to follow someone else through the stages of creating a presentation.

In this Step you'll see how a fictional presenter, Susan Alexander, director of marketing for the sample company ComputerEase, builds some of the slides of her PowerPoint presentation using both basic and more advanced techniques.

For the basis of this presentation, Susan uses the core message, organisation and notes she developed in Steps 2 and 3 of this book. For the complete presentation text, see pages 58–59.

Keep in mind that Susan may create additional slides. This Step is designed to show you how to create the fundamental slides you'll need and then add some bells and whistles to give your presentation punch.

QUICK**TIP**

**Making the Transition**

PowerPoint gives you the opportunity to create dynamic transitions between slides, but these are generally too distracting for business presentations. Check them out by going to the **Slide Show** menu on the top toolbar, then selecting **Slide Transition**.

# Slide 1: Set up the show and create title slide

First, Susan will set up the look of her slides. She has chosen to do this using a standard PowerPoint design template.

Here's how to start:

1. Click on the pulldown menu of the right-hand task pane. The first time you open PowerPoint, it will be titled **Getting Started**.

2. Click and select **New Presentation**.

3. Click **From design template**. Thumbnail versions of several slide design templates will then appear in the pane under the words **Apply a design template**.

4. Choose and click an appropriate design. That design will automatically appear on the slide you see and all slides in your presentation. (You can also go to Microsoft Office Online for additional slide designs.)

*Note: You can easily change the design of your slides at any time—just return to the **Slide Design** task pane and click on a different design.*

Susan selects a design from the available templates in the right-hand task pane. The design then shows up on the slide in the centre window of her screen. Her first slide then looks like this:

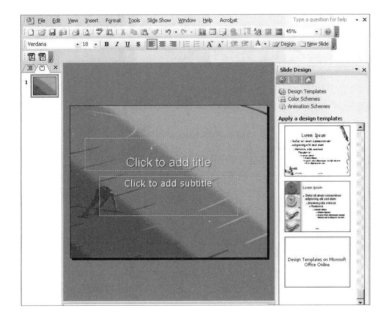

To create a title slide, Susan inserts her text into the text boxes on the slide template in the centre, moving from one text box to the other with her mouse.

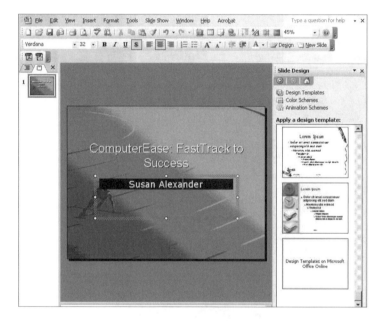

She decides to make some adjustments to the size, colour, and placement of the text. To do so, she clicks within the text boxes and then manipulates text just as she would in any Microsoft Word document. In this case, Susan converts the subtitle to italics, changes its colour and centres it on the screen.

Here's how title slide now looks:

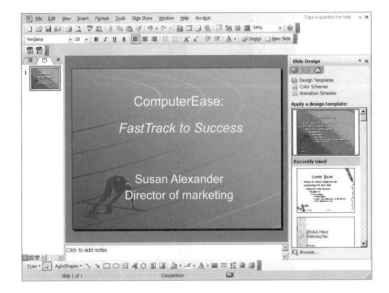

Susan will keep this slide on the screen while she waits for her audience to enter the room and settle in for her presentation.

# Slide 2: Add emphasis with text animation

Susan wants the next slide of her presentation to grab her audience's attention. This slide will appear on screen while she delivers her opening hook.

To give the hook even greater impact, Susan wants her text to appear on the screen one line at a time, rather than all at once. To do this, she will use **Animation**.

In most cases, you'll want to use very subtle types of PowerPoint **Animation**, as Susan does in this sample presentation. When used by PowerPoint, the term **Animation** doesn't mean the same thing as it does when used by Disney. In Power-Point, **Animation** refers to how text (or an image) appears, disappears, or moves around on the screen.

PowerPoint provides you with a number of pre-designed **Animation Schemes**. Resist the temptation to add very active, or as PowerPoint calls them, **Exciting**, animation schemes. They're too distracting for most business presentations.

**Opening Statement**

*£520,000. That's what Widget Solutions threw away last year on outside emergency tech support for problems that should have been handled in-house. £520,000 for computer problems that could have been easily resolved by your existing employees, had they been equipped with the proper training. And that doesn't even address the costs of employee down time, the time and money that slipped away as staff waited for someone else to come in and fix their machines.*

To create a slide that incorporates **Animation**, first enter your text (or image):

1. Click the **New Slide** button on the upper right side of the toolbar menu.

2. Choose the **Slide Layout** design that best suits the way you want text (and/or other images) to appear on your slide.

3. Type your text in the appropriate areas on the slide.

On her slide, Susan types in the title, *'Cost of IT Services',* and in the text box, she places two key concepts from her opening statement:

- £520,000

- Plus costs of down time

Susan decides to:

● Change the size and colour of the text and centre some of it by using the format toolbar at the top of the screen. (These are the same techniques she'd use in Microsoft Word.) She also deletes the bullet points that PowerPoint automatically inserted.

Notice that in the **Notes** section below the centre window, Susan places notes about the opening part of the written presentation she prepared earlier. This is to remind herself of what she wants to say.

Susan uses as little text as possible on the slide itself. That's so her slides will be easy for her audience to grasp and will reinforce the most important parts of her spoken presentation.

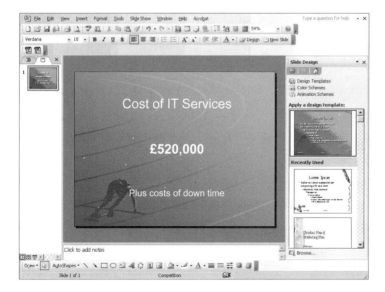

To add emphasis to her opening hook, Susan decides to use text **Animation**.

By using a PowerPoint **Animation Scheme**, Susan can better control when text appears on screen. Susan wants her audience to remember the number '£520,000', so she wants that to appear on screen before the other text. To make this happen, she sets up her presentation so that each line on this slide appears separately.

Here are two ways to accomplish this. First, the easy way:

1. If you've closed out the **Design** task pane, click the **Design** button on the toolbar to make the **Slide Design** task pane appear.

2. In the **Slide Design** pane, click **Animation Schemes**. You will see a long list of options.

3. Choose **Fade in one by one** to make each line of your text appear as you click ahead.

4. Preview the effect by clicking **Slide Show** at the bottom of the right-hand task pane.

You will now see each line of type fade in individually as you click ahead while the presentation is showing.

The downside of using the easy way is that every line of text, including the title, will be animated. What if you don't want your slide title to fade in, or you want only certain lines to fade in while others remain static?

1. Click on the **Slide Show** pulldown menu on the toolbar at the top of your screen.

2. Select **Custom Animation**.

3. Highlight the text you want to animate, in the order you want the animation to occur. For example, Susan wants '£520,000' to appear first, so she highlights it first.

4. Click and hold the **Add Effect** button. While still holding, slide your cursor to the left, onto **Entrance**. Choose your effect. (If you want your text to appear quickly, choose **Appear**. If you want it to show up more gradually, choose **Fade**.)

5. After that's done, select the next line of text you wish to animate and repeat the process.

6. To preview the effect, click the **Slide Show** button at the bottom of the **Custom Animation** window.

   *Note: To get out of **Slide Show** mode, right click anywhere on the screen while you're in it and select **End Show**.*

You now have a slide that underscores the concepts you want to reinforce. Susan added impact to the amount of money the potential client, Widget Solutions, spent on IT services last year—an amount they could have saved with the help of ComputerEase.

# Slide 3: Animate bullet points

Susan decides to use a similar animation scheme on the bullet points in her next slide to reinforce one of the main arguments in her presentation.

### Sample script

*The unique training programme developed and tested by ComputerEase can significantly enhance the skill sets of your employees. We can equip them with the knowledge and tools needed to resolve the basic technical problems that occur on a day-to-day basis. That means you save money and you and your team can get back to work.*

First, Susan creates a new slide and enters her text. To do so:

1. Click on **New Slide** in the upper right-hand corner of the screen.

2. Choose the **Slide Layout** that is most appropriate for your text and/or images. In this case, Susan uses the default slide layout.

3. Enter the text.

Then, using the same animation as in the previous slide—either choosing **Animation Schemes** or **Custom Animation**—Susan sets up the slide so she can make each bullet point appear as she clicks ahead. This enables her to control exactly when her audience sees the text of each point she wants to make.

(To preview your choices, click the **Slide Show** button on the **Design** task pane.)

In the **Notes** section below the centre window, Susan once again types or pastes her script as a way to help prompt her as she gives her spoken presentation. If you don't find this helpful, it's not necessary.

# Slide 4: Add charts and graphics

Since Susan has already shown her audience three text-based slides (including her title), she decides to make her presentation more visually interesting by adding a graphic element.

Susan has a chart in her files that shows how ComputerEase training increases employees' efficiency, the next argument she wants to make in her presentation.

### Sample Text

*ComputerEase enhances your employees' efficiency by 50 per cent.*

- ● *Subpoint: Proven in tests with client user groups.*
- ● *Subpoint: Better than sending employees to off-site training programmes. We come to you. (Keeps employees on-site.)*
- ● *Subpoint: Employees don't waste time waiting around for tech support. They learn how to quickly resolve problems themselves and get back to work.*

To add a chart, or other image from your files, to a presentation:

1. Click the **New Slide** button in the upper right-hand corner to open a new slide.

2. Choose the **Slide Layout** that best approximates how you want the text and the image to appear on your finished slide.

3. Place the cursor over the slide and click where you wish to insert the chart or other graphic element. (You may be prompted to click to add content, clip art, charts, or media clips. Ignore those prompts for the time being and follow the procedure below.)

4. Click on the **Insert** pulldown menu in your top toolbar.

5. Select and hold down **Picture**, then select **From File**.

6. Navigate through your files (as you would with any other programme) until you find the chart, graphic, photo, or image you want to use. Double click the image. It should appear on your slide.

7. You'll then almost certainly need to adjust your graphic.

8. Resize your chart or other image by moving around until you get a **sizing handle** at a corner or side (see page 118). Hover over one of the sizing handles until you see the two-sided arrow tool, then hold down to resize.

9. Reposition the image on your slide by moving your cursor around until you see the four-point arrow tool (see page 118). Right click and hold to move the image.

Use the same procedure to insert any stored image into your presentation and manipulate it on your slide.

Susan's simple chart will be seen by her audience while she discusses the results of the efficiency study. The visual and spoken aspects of the presentation complement each other, helping the audience realise the significance of her argument.

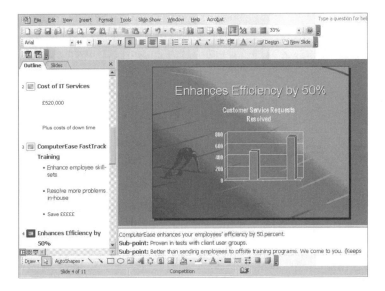

QUICK**TIP**

**Use Charts to Simplify Numbers**

Charts, graphs and other linear graphics help your audience grasp the significance of numerical data. A bar chart works well for comparisons, as when showing sales of two different products, or for a Before and After view of test subjects. Graphs can be used to illustrate changes over a period of time. Pie charts are helpful when showing proportions or percentages.

# Slide 5: Combine photos with text and use stock photos

Like charts or graphs, photos can break up the monotony of text slides. They add colour and liveliness to a presentation. Most importantly, they can communicate concepts more clearly and with far more emotional impact than text.

When Susan created her chart slide, you saw how to retrieve an image from your files, insert it into your slide and then re-size or move it. (See page 168.)

If you don't have an image of your own that you want to use, you can also use the **Insert** menu to retrieve photos from Microsoft Office Clip Art file or through Microsoft Office Online, as Susan will do for this slide.

**Note:** PowerPoint includes a selection of *royalty-free* clip art—photos, drawings, movies, music—that you can include in your presentations. You can find them both through the PowerPoint programme or by connecting to the Microsoft Office Online website.

Susan has now reached the final argument in the body of her presentation. She wants to emphasise the connection between a better-trained staff and loyal customers. To do so, she finds a stock photo of a happy customer service representative to add to her slide. This will convey a positive emotion while adding visual interest.

**Sample Text**

*A better-trained staff enhances the performance and value of your company.*

- *Subpoint: Employees can better assist customers, increasing customer loyalty and repeat business.*
- *Subpoint: Employees overcome problems more easily, allowing your company to get on with the business of making money.*
- *Subpoint: More employee confidence and higher job satisfaction translates to lower staff turnover and a more stable company.*

To add a stock photo to a slide:

1. Click the **New Slide** button in the upper right-hand side of the toolbar menu.

2. Scroll down the **Slide layout** task pane to find an appropriate layout for your slide. In this case, Susan scrolls down and makes a selection under **Other Layouts**.

You can double click to add clip art and then search for an appropriate image, but that brings up illustrations as well as photos. Instead:

1. Click on the **Insert** pull-down menu in your top toolbar.

2. Select and hold down **Picture**, then select **Clip Art**. A **Clip Art** task pane now opens in the right-hand column.

3. In the box under the words **Results should be:** there appears a pulldown menu with the words **Selected media file types**. Use the pulldown menu to select **Photographs**.

4. In the box under the words **Search for:** enter a word that describes the kind of image you're looking for or some aspect of that image. You may have to try a number of words related to your general concept to find an appropriate image. Susan uses the term 'headset' to find a photo that depicts a customer service representative.

5. If you can't find an image you like, scroll down to **Clip art on Office Online** to see more photos available from Microsoft's Office website.

6. Navigate through the photos until you find the one you want to use. Double click the image. It should appear on your slide. You'll then almost certainly need to adjust the size of your photo.

7. Resize your photo by moving your cursor around until you get a **sizing handle** at a corner or side. Hover over one of the sizing handles until you see the two-sided arrow tool, then hold down to resize.

8. Reposition the photo on your slide so that you can still add text in a text box. Move your cursor around on the photo until you see the four-point arrow tool. Right click and hold to move.

## QUICK**TIP**

### Working with Image Files

To keep your PowerPoint file size as small as possible, use images in JPEG or GIF formats. GIF format works best for line art (like charts); JPEG is best for photos. Avoid BMP, TIFF and PNG files, which are large.

Next, you'll want to add text to your slide:

● Click inside the text box. Susan then adds the three subpoints that illustrate her main argument.

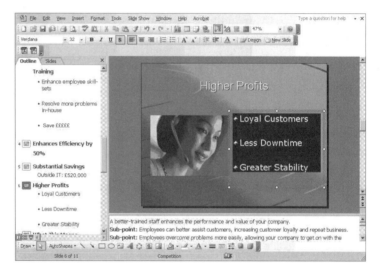

## Slide 6: Use unaccompanied photos to reinforce themes

Susan is now ready to set up the transition to her closing, where she'll review the main points she has made thus far.

**Sample Text**

*These are just a few of the ways we can help your company. Our current clients have reported many more benefits, such as smoother workflow processes, stronger relationships with strategic partners and an increase in new ideas and product innovations originating from the employees we've trained.*

At this point, Susan wants her audience to listen to her, rather than read words on a screen. She also wants to create positive emotional associations with ComputerEase and employee training while she continues to build her case.

To do this, Susan has decided to display a simple photo of employees at a training session while she delivers the transition to her closing remarks.

### Where to Find Sounds and Pictures

Images, audio clips and short videos can add life to your presentation. But where do you find them? Here are several sites offering free or low-cost files. Be sure to check usage policies on each site before downloading:

| IMAGES | AUDIO | VIDEO | VARIOUS |
|---|---|---|---|
| bigfoto.com | freeaudioclips.com | animationfactory.com | Microsoft Office Online (office.microsoft.com; linked directly to PowerPoint) |
| corbis.com | findsounds.com | freestockfootage.com | |
| freefoto.com | wavplanet.com | | PCWorld.com/downloads (under Graphics & Multi-media, choose from audio, images and video) |
| geekphilosopher.com | wavsource.com | | |
| jupiterimages.com | | | |
| microsoft.com | | | |

Placing a photo on a blank slide is fairly simple:

1. Click the **New Slide** button in the upper right side of the toolbar menu.

2. In the **Slide Layout** task pane, under **Content Layouts**, select the blank slide layout.

3. Click on the **Insert** pulldown menu in your top toolbar.

4. Select and hold down **Picture**, then select either **Clip Art** or **From File**. Select the photo you want to use either from your files or from stock photos as described in the previous section.

5. Resize and reposition the photo as needed.

## Slide 7: Insert audio files

To strengthen her company's credibility, Susan has decided to use a customer testimonial as part of her presentation.

In addition to her own remarks, Susan had previously asked a satisfied corporate client to tape an audio testimonial about ComputerEase. She will use this to enhance a slide at the close of her presentation.

**Sample Text**

*Here's what our customers have to say about our innovative training methods:*

*Client's Voice: 'Our staff has been training with ComputerEase for just under two months. We've already saved thousands of pounds on outside IT repair costs. Employee morale is much better, too. It's simply a great programme.'*

Susan already has a photo of her customer and a digital recording of the testimonial she wants to use in the presentation.

She inserts and adjusts the photo in the same way she did for her photo slides.

*Note: If you're trying to complete your presentation in a day, it's best to use photos and audio already saved to your files rather than trying to create new ones when you're pressured for time.*

To insert an audio clip:

1. Click the place on the side where you want the clip inserted.

2. From the **Insert** pulldown menu, select and hold down **Movies and Sounds**. You can add audio and video clips from files on your computer, the Microsoft Clip Organiser, a network or intranet, or the Internet.

3. Select the source of your audio clip.

4. Once you find it, double click it to insert it into your presentation.

This same method is used to insert video clips.

Susan creates her slide and plays the audio by clicking on the audio icon 🔊 with her cursor (when in **Slide Show** mode):

# Slide 8: Animate photos

Susan is now ready to deliver her closing. To help her audience remember her core message, Susan brings back the attention-getter she used at the beginning of her presentation.

She wants to drive home her point about the value of her company's services using attractive images of other ways her client could use £520,000 in savings. She finds stock images representing new office space, new computer equipment and happy employees.

She then incorporates them into her slide using the same **Custom Animation** scheme she's used previously when animating text (see page 165):

1. Click the **New Slide** button in the upper right side of the toolbar menu and choose an appropriate layout, probably a blank slide.

2. Using the **Insert** menu, go to **Picture** and retrieve your photos (from your files, clip art collection, or online).

3. Place the photos as you'd like them to be positioned on your slide.

4. Under the **Slide Show** menu, select **Custom Animation**. The **Custom Animation** task pane appears on the right side of your screen.

5. On your slide, click the photo you want to appear first.

6. Click **Add Effect**, then move the cursor over **Entrance** and select **Appear**.

7. Follow this procedure with the next two photos, in order of desired appearance.

**Hint:** If you overlay your photos and have trouble getting the one you want to appear on top, simply cut and then repaste it. The photo inserted last is the one that appears on top.

Susan has set up her animation scheme so she can make each photo appear on cue as she presses her arrow keys.

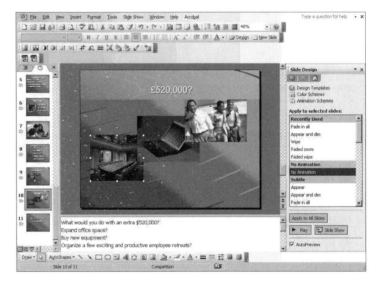

***Susan's slide (in* Normal *mode).*** *The photos appear one by one as Susan clicks ahead, allowing her to emphasise her points.*

## Slide 9: Create final slide

Susan has completed her presentation and is now ready for questions from her audience. During her question-and-answer session and any concluding remarks, Susan leaves a slide on screen containing the name of her company, the title of her presentation, her name and contact information.

Don't turn your slide show off the minute you finish your presentation. Instead create a final slide with key information and leave it on the screen throughout your question-and-answer session. This makes it easy for audience members to write down your contact information and remember your name.

# Pulling It All Together: Enhancing Your Presentation

Susan created her winning presentation using a PowerPoint template, basic text manipulation skills and a few other relatively easy-to-learn PowerPoint techniques. With a careful balance of text, graphics, animation and sound, she developed a visual display that:

- Complements, rather than competes with, her spoken presentation

- Engages her audience

- Is emotionally appealling to her audience

- Drives home the key points of her message

For additional PowerPoint tips and help, go to Microsoft Office Online (***www.office.microsoft.com***) and click **Assistance** in the left navigation bar. You'll find the link to PowerPoint assistance about halfway down the main page.

# Troubleshooting:
## When Good Presentations Go Bad

Sooner or later, something is going to go wrong. You may arrive at your event only to find your computer won't work, your handouts have been lost, or you've got to cut your sixty-minute presentation down to ten.

Benjamin Franklin once said, 'An ounce of prevention is worth a pound of cure.' That's certainly true when it comes to ensuring that everything goes right for your winning presentation. Taking a few simple precautionary measures in advance can eliminate most of the things that can happen during your presentation. If you want to feel like absolutely everything went right, prepare for the fact that anything can go wrong.

In this section, you'll learn about potential presentation problems and how to prevent or recover from them. With a little preparation and a bit of quick thinking, even if something goes wrong, you can still give a winning presentation.

## QUICK**TIP**

### Arrive Early

The overwhelming majority of problems can be solved if you have the time to deal with them. Should you arrive just five or ten minutes before your presentation begins and discover something's gone wrong, it's much less likely you'll be able to fix it.

# Technical problems

## PROBLEM:
## Your computer doesn't work.

### Prevention:

- Bring an extra copy of your PowerPoint presentation or other necessary data on a removable disk that can be used on someone else's computer.

- Email a copy of your PowerPoint slides to a conference organiser in advance.

- Bring handouts containing the key points of your presentation that can be distributed when you speak.

### At the last minute:

- Restart your computer.

- Make sure everything is plugged in.

- Take a deep breath and wing it; lots of people give great presentations without computers.

## PROBLEM:
## There's no projector available for your PowerPoint slides.

### Prevention:

- Double check ahead of time that a projector has been ordered.

- Bring handouts containing the key points of your presentation that can be distributed when you speak.

### At the last minute:

- Try to round up a projector from another room.

- Rent a projector from an AV company.

- Take a deep breath and wing it without slides.

## PROBLEM:
## The computer blocks you from the view of the audience.

### Prevention:

- Bring an extension cord, or order one in advance from your event organiser, so you can move your computer.

- Bring a remote control to advance the slides so you can move around the room.

### At the last minute:

- Ask a member of the audience or the event organiser to run the computer for you and advance the slides when you indicate.

## PROBLEM:
## The room is large and there's no microphone.

### Prevention:

- Double check with your event organiser to make sure that they've ordered a mike.

- Prepare a PowerPoint or other slide presentation; listeners will understand more if they can see what you're talking about, even if they can't hear you well.

### At the last minute:

- Move around the room as you speak; be careful not to turn your back to listeners.

## Room setup

**PROBLEM:**
**The speakers' podium is located far from the audience.**

**Prevention:**

● Request a different room setup from the event organiser in advance.

● If the setup can't be changed, request a radio microphone so you can move around the room.

**At the last minute:**

● Stand closer to your listeners, even if it means you can't use the mike.

● Increase the size of your gestures and raise your energy level to help bridge the gap between you and the audience.

● See if you can rearrange the room.

**PROBLEM:**
**The room is too big.**

**Prevention:**

● Ask your event organiser in advance about the size of the room and anticipated audience. If necessary, request a more appropriately sized room.

**At the last minute:**

● Remove extra chairs from the back of the room.

● Ask your event organiser to rope off parts of the room.

● Ask listeners to move to the front of the room.

## PROBLEM:
## The room is too small.

### Prevention:

- Ask your event organiser in advance about the size of the room and anticipated audience. If necessary, request a more appropriately sized room.

### At the last minute:

- Ask your event organiser for another room.

- Add chairs.

- If possible, lower the temperature in the room; packed rooms get very warm.

## PROBLEM:
## You've got to compete with outside noises, clanging dishes, or music from the building's audio system.

### Prevention:

- Request a microphone, even in a small room.

- Prepare a PowerPoint or other slide presentation; listeners will understand more if they can see what you're talking about, even if they can't hear you well.

### At the last minute:

- See if the audio system can be turned off.

- Thank the waiting staff and audience for being as quiet as possible while you speak as a hint for them to keep the noise down.

- Speak loudly, even with a mike.

# Audience

**PROBLEM:**
**Very few people show up.**

**Prevention:**

- Come up with an enticing title for your presentation.

- Email invitees to let them know about your presentation.

- Interview a few potential attendees about your topic in advance; these folks will then be more likely to show up.

**At the last minute:**

- Ask everyone to move closer together.

- Give those who do show up your very best.

**PROBLEM:**
**No one shows up.**

**Prevention:**

- Come up with an enticing title for your presentation.

- Email invitees to let them know about your presentation.

- Interview a few potential attendees about your topic in advance; these folks will then be more likely to show up.

**At the last minute:**

- Have a cup of coffee and soothe your bruised ego. Those people don't know what they missed!

## PROBLEM:
## The audience knows much more or much less about the topic than you had anticipated.

### Prevention:

- Ask the event organiser in advance to tell you as much about the audience as possible.

- Interview a few potential attendees about your topic in advance. That will give you a better idea of how much they know about the topic.

### At the last minute:

- At the beginning of your presentation, take a quick poll to determine how much your audience knows about the topic.

- If possible, adjust your presentation to the knowledge level of the audience.

## PROBLEM:
## A competitor is in the audience.

### Prevention:

- Ask the event organiser to tell you who will be in the audience.

- Be careful not to reveal any proprietary or confidential information.

### At the last minute:

- Take a deep breath and give the best presentation you can.

- If your competitor asks a question about proprietary matters or makes a hostile comment, make it clear that this person is your competitor and don't feel compelled to respond in depth. Your audience will be sympathetic.

**PROBLEM:
An audience member makes an antagonistic comment or asks a hostile question.**

**Prevention:**

- Ask the event organiser in advance to tell you who will be in the audience.

**At the last minute:**

- Thank the person for sharing their point of view. Then turn the comment or question back to the core message of your presentation: *'I can appreciate that you feel that way, but the facts don't support you. As I was saying…'*

- Do not get sucked into responding or creating a dialogue with this person. That only gives them more attention and detracts from your authority.

**PROBLEM:
A questioner rambles on and on.**

**Prevention:**

- Hold onto the microphone when letting someone ask a question. That way you can slowly draw it back from them when they go on for too long.

- Have audience members submit questions on index cards.

- If there's a moderator, ask the moderator in advance to cut off the long-winded.

**At the last minute:**

- Nod, and interrupt with a positive comment such as *'I see what you're getting at…'* and then respond briefly.

## PROBLEM:
## A member of the audience points out a mistake you've made.

### Prevention:

- Double check your facts.

### At the last minute:

- Thank the person for the correction. Don't get flustered; everyone makes mistakes. If you respond with dignity, you can still maintain your authority.

# Miscellaneous

**PROBLEM:**
**Your presentation time has been dramatically cut.**

**Prevention:**

- Double check with your event organiser about the amount of time you have for your presentation.

- Organise your presentation using the *building* structure as outlined in Step 3. That way, you'll easily be able to cut subpoints and still retain your core message and call to action.

**At the last minute:**

- Focus on the things you most want your audience to remember—your core message and call to action. Eliminate your PowerPoint presentation.

- If you have time, use the **Slide Sorter** view in your PowerPoint presentation. Right click on slides you don't have time to show your audience and select **Hide Slide**.

**PROBLEM:**
**Your presentation time has been dramatically increased.**

**Prevention:**

- Double check with your event organiser about the amount of time you have for your presentation.

- Organise your presentation using the *building* structure as discussed in Step 3 and add additional subpoints you've prepared in advance.

- Interview a few members of the audience in advance so you can call on some of them to share their experiences, if appropriate.

**At the last minute:**

- Expand the amount of time for questions and answers.

- Take a bit longer to make each main argument or subpoint; use a few more examples.

## PROBLEM:
**Every other presenter has a PowerPoint presentation except you.**

**Prevention:**

- Ask your event organiser in advance what is expected of you and what other presenters are doing.

**At the last minute:**

- Take a deep breath. Be as interesting and dynamic as possible. Remember, for centuries people gave compelling presentations without PowerPoint.

## PROBLEM:
**Your handouts or other materials are missing.**

**Prevention:**

- Send them to the event organiser well in advance.

- Double check with the event organiser that they've arrived.

- Send them to your hotel rather than the conference hotel or event organiser.

- Bring them with you.

- Bring a master copy of all your materials so you can have them duplicated at the last minute if necessary.

- Have key points on PowerPoint slides.

**At the last minute:**

- Print out a new master copy of your handouts and get duplicates made.

- Ask attendees to write responses or complete exercises on plain paper.

- Skip the portion of your presentation that requires handouts.

# Troubleshooting Checklist

One of the most effective ways to prevent problems is to identify them in advance. Use this checklist to help you prepare for your presentation.

## Equipment/Supplies

☐ Make certain you've brought your laptop and power cord

☐ Bring extra battery for your laptop

☐ Bring backup PowerPoint files (on storage media)

☐ Email a copy of your PowerPoint slides to event organiser

☐ Bring backup 35mm slides or transparencies (if using these)

☐ Bring extension cord

☐ Double check with organiser that projector has been ordered

☐ Request a lapel or hand-held mike

☐ Double check with organiser that microphone has been ordered

☐ Double check with organiser that any other AV equipment will be available

☐ Bring extra whiteboard markers

☐ Bring electrical tape

☐ Double check that your handouts have arrived

☐ Bring master copy of your handouts

☐ Find location of copy store nearest your event venue in advance

☐ Bring plenty of business cards

## Audience/Venue

☐ Ask event organiser about the nature and number of attendees

☐ Interview a few potential attendees in advance; ask event organiser for names and contact info

☐ Ask organiser about the size and arrangement of the room

☐ Request a glass of water at podium

☐ Bring a bottle of water

## Appearance

☐ Bring extra tie and/or backup outfit

☐ Empty your pockets of bulky items

☐ Bring breath mints

☐ Check self in the mirror before presenting

## At the venue, check to make sure

☐ All the plugs are plugged in

☐ All the switches are turned on

☐ The sound level of your microphone is appropriate

☐ All your equipment is working

☐ The room temperature is adjusted for the number of people in the room

☐ Your handouts are distributed

☐ The proper number of chairs are in the room for expected attendance

☐ You can be seen by all members of the audience from where you're going to stand

# The Experts Talk

Wouldn't it be wonderful if you could enter the minds of the people who give presentations for a living—if you could learn what works, what doesn't, and how they make every presentation a winning one?

Now you can. On the following pages, you'll find interviews with expert speakers and a PowerPoint product manager.

They'll tell you in their own words:

- The best—and worst—ways to use PowerPoint during a presentation

- What are the most common mistakes that presenters make

- What kind of body language is the most effective during a presentation

- How to make the best use of your notes while presenting

Before you make your presentation, learn from the experts interviewed here. Use their real-life experience to help you prepare for and give your presentation. Their insights into everything from how many slides to create (the answer may surprise you) to how to handle 'showboating' will help you create a winning presentation every time.

## Chris Lewis: MD of Lewis PR

*A journalist by training, Chris has driven a decade of growth and profitability to create an employee-owned multi-million pound global communications business, with 35 offices internationally. Chris has travelled the globe evangelising British media. He has ten years' experience of coaching senior politicians and business leaders.*

*He has written two top selling books on business:* The Unemployables *(1994) and* Brilliant Minds *(1997) and continues to contribute to national and international press.*

*Chris began his career in Fleet Street during the News International dispute at Wapping. Combining an impressive financial background and writing ability, Chris went on to work for a variety of national and international press including* The Times, Financial Times, Daily Telegraph, Guardian, *plus many trade titles.*

---

### What are some characteristics of an effective presentation?

Remember that a presentation competes for attention. In a world that has multi-channel TV, DVD, Wii, Internet, etc., attention spans are getting shorter.

BUT presentations can still compete. Provided they are visual. Ninety per cent of any message is VISUAL. That's why eye contact is important. So is animation. Flickering, unfocused or incomplete eye contact can completely change meaning. It should also be spontaneous and simple. It also helps if it is structured, legible, concise and funny. Nothing is more frustrating than listening to the 3Ms – muddle, mumble and monotone.

### What are some of the most common mistakes people make?

Not rehearsing.

Not using enough pictures.

Not getting the audience on side at the start. For example, try saying 'Thank you for making the time to listen. I'm pleased to be here. I'll only be twenty minutes. Do stop me and buy one.' Etc. etc. Empathy and rapport is the name of the game.

Death by PowerPoint. The software is the magician's assistant, not the magician. Debbie McGee, not Paul Daniels.

People buy from people not PowerPoint.

Reading the slides out loud.

Covering too many points on each page. Not being animated. Using clip art.

Not being spontaneous when making a mistake. All too frequently, people only pay attention when something goes wrong.

The best mistakes are the funniest – wardrobe malfunctions, farting and falling off stage, all rank among the best.

### What are some of the less obvious problems you've encountered in your presentations or seen in others?

Technical failure is always the one nobody anticipates. The file could never corrupt could it? The speakers are bound to work. You'll have the right cable. Of course you will.

Will the slides advance when you click the mouse? Familiarise yourself with technology especially if it is someone else's.

Being attacked by a wasp, catching the seat of your trousers on a door catch, fainting, breaking the furniture.

Most problems track to poor planning. Time spent on reconnaissance is seldom wasted. What size if the room? How will I get there? How long will I have? Who will I follow?

### How should you stand or move on stage during a presentation?

The biggest factor is whether the speaker is using a microphone and where it is. If it's a desk or rostrum mike then they must stay static. If it's a lapel mike they can roam. But too much movement is distracting. Stand still to make a point. Be aware of lighting. All too frequently a speaker will step outside a pool of light.

### When you're at a panel discussion, how should you sit? Where should you look?

Always look at the speaker or the questioner. Sit up straight, leaning slightly forward with your hands in front of you. Be aware that leaning back looks disinterested and lacks enthusiasm. Try to avoid scratching any part of your body.

### What is effective eye contact?

Paradoxically, never in the eyes, but always on the bridge of the nose or forehead. Someone else's gaze can easily distract. One to one it should be consistent 4–5 seconds at any one time. To a crowd, it should be 4–5 seconds in each corner then in the centre.

### Should you smile during your presentation?

Yes. Smile, frown, purse, gape – anything to make it animated and visual.

Obviously, don't smile if you're making a serious point – people will think you're an imbecile.

### What do you do when someone asks a long question that never seems to end, or wants to ask more questions or engage with you when you've already answered them once?

Ask the audience if anyone else has this issue. Very seldom will people respond immediately. Then ask if you can take it off-line so you can cover it in greater detail. Ask if the person minds if some other people ask a question so you can address their concerns, too.

### What kinds of notes do you use?

I try not to use any in favour of spatial memory. This involves picking out the key words, then arranging them visually in a journey. It makes complex speeches easy. Notes impact a presentation in three ways. Firstly, they disrupt eye contact. Secondly, they direct the voice down and into the notes. Thirdly, they tend to inhibit use of the hands.

### Do you use PowerPoint in your presentations? (Give reasons)

Yes. To explain diagrams, pictures and simply words. Perhaps also to play video. Beware using PowerPoint to structure presentations. Always draft out the presentation on paper as an argument.

PowerPoint presentations must make sense as stand-alone items, because they are often forwarded via email.

# Nova Ferguson: Learning Consultant, QA-IQ

*Nova has been working with UK learning company QA-IQ for nearly ten years, developing and delivering training programmes to improve interpersonal and management skills. She has worked on training programmes for major corporate customers running workshops covering presentation skills, facilitation, influencing and assertiveness, mentoring skills and time management.*

*Nova has extensive experience of training in the insurance, purchasing and procurement, public health, IT and banking sectors, and has experience of learning programmes ranging from developing and delivering bespoke training plans to large organisations to providing one-to-one coaching to managers.*

*With a range of management experience working in both the public and private sectors, Nova has spent five years working in UK local government and fourteen years working in the private sector. She is an NLP Master Practitioner and qualified SDI Facilitator*

### What are some characteristics of an effective presentation?

An effective presentation makes real contact with the audience. The presenter understands the profile of their audience and what will appeal to them. An effective presenter is having a conversation with their audience. A presenter's main concern should be how the audience is responding, and whether they are happy, rather than how you as presenter are performing.

An effective presentation is clear-cut in outlining the benefits of the presentation for the audience. Why are they there? How can they benefit from what they are about to hear? And what actions should they take as a result of what they learn?

### What are some of the most common mistakes people make?

The most common mistake is delivering information from the presenter's perspective – presenting what's in it for you rather than what's in it for your audience. Presenters should not make assumptions about the prior knowledge of their audience, and shouldn't presume what they need to know.

Contingency planning is essential, and often overlooked. In particular, plan for changes to the timing. What will you do if a previous presentation runs over and you need to dramatically shorten yours? Or if you need to fill a gap at the end of your session?

You should also check the physical environment before the presentation; make sure it's suitable and make sure that the equipment is working. Plan some alternatives so you can cope if there are technical problems.

### What are some of the less obvious problems you've encountered in your presentations or seen in others?

A less obvious problem is a lack of knowledge about the language capability of the audience. This can include using large amounts of jargon with a non-technical audience, or using idioms – particularly with an international audience. You need to be able to cater to greater or lesser levels of fluency in the language in which you are presenting.

However hard you prepare there are some things that are beyond your control. You need to be able to take in good spirit any unforeseen setbacks and not let it colour the whole presentation. For example, when checking equipment, check pens as well as computers; despite being an experienced presenter I have managed to poke myself in the eye with a pen, as well as covering myself with ink from a broken marker. A colleague also stood up to present a piece on appearance with his shirt tail visible through his trouser fly.

### How should you stand or move on stage during a presentation?

If you're going to move while presenting you need to ensure that you move for a relevant purpose; that fits with what you're saying. Some people pace up and down, hoping to burn off nervous energy, but this doesn't work and can be distracting for the audience. Using a contrast of movement, stillness and movement is effective, and sometimes you need to understand and accept that it's OK to be still.

### When you're at a panel discussion, how should you sit? Where should you look?

It's important to make sure that you can make eye contact with each member of the panel and with as much of the audience as you can. When a question is asked, make eye contact with the questioner for about three seconds at the start of your answer, then move on to look at the rest of the group or audience.

You should sit with your backside firmly tucked in to the curve of seat, and your shoulders dropped not high. This allows you to sit on a straight spine, which not only looks more 'present' but also allows better flow of oxygen to brain keeping you more alert.

### What is effective eye contact?

Always remember that appropriate and effective eye contact depends on the culture of those to whom you're presenting. In Western cultures three to five seconds is ideal. You should hold eye contact with an individual for long enough to tell them your idea – people sitting around them will also feel that you're looking at them during this time.

### Should you smile during your presentation?

You shouldn't be afraid to smile if it's appropriate to what you're saying. However, only smile if you're comfortable with it; if you're uncomfortable it will look strange.

Remember that part of your task as a good presenter is to help the audience to relax – audiences get anxious when presenters are nervous. An audience will subconsciously pick up on a presenter's breathing patterns and will be uncomfortable with the content of your presentation if you are uncomfortable in your delivery.

### What do you do when someone asks a long question that never seems to end, or wants to ask more questions or engage with you when you've already answered them once?

You should take the question, but then step back to include your whole audience. With a very long question you should paraphrase the question, or ask the questioner to rephrase it more concisely; often people ask long questions to present their own agenda.

Once you begin answering the question you should make eye contact with someone in another part of the room – don't look back at the questioner and at the end of your answer clearly invite other members of the audience to ask further questions or contribute.

Don't return to the questioner to ask 'Is that alright?' or 'Does that answer your question?' as this is an invitation for further input from them.

### What kinds of notes do you use?

The type of notes really depends on the individual. I use mind maps – for a familiar presentation it will be an A4 sheet, and for a new presentation on A3. I will prop this on a chair, if possible to the bottom right of where I'm standing. This allows me to glance at my notes without creating a barrier with the audience.

Index cards are also popular, but make sure if you're using text that you stick to bullet points, and don't get 'lost' in the body of the text.

### Do you use PowerPoint in your presentations? (Give reasons)

Yes, I do use PowerPoint; often because it's expected in a corporate environment. A presenter's strongest visual aid is themselves, so switching media from PowerPoint to flip charts, to speaking directly to the audience, will keep their attention. It goes without saying that you should strictly limit the number of slides used in PowerPoint, and don't use it if you aren't comfortable with the technology.

# John Donnelly: Self-Employed Motivational Speaker

*John Donnelly is an experienced presenter and author. Having spent many years scrutinising the most effective business leaders in the UK – the business rainmakers – his research-based approach to business training has made him one of the most sought after keynote speakers in the business.*

*Once described as a Mancunian version of Sir John Harvey Jones, Donnelly insists that even the best content has to have 'stick-ability and survive the delegate's journey back to their real world. "You have to earn the right to teach" was Jim Henson's motto (originator of* Sesame Street *and* The Muppet Show*) and he helped a whole generation to read and write!'*

*He has worked with companies like HP, Dixons, 3M and the IOD.*

### What are some characteristics of an effective presentation?

Firstly, you need to do your homework properly; you need to give the audience what they want to know, not what you want to say. And you have to give it to them in the right sequence for them. The aim is not just to present, you've got to blow their bloody socks off!

Humour is also important because whilst they're laughing, they're learning … lots! But the humour has got to be built in, not bolted on.

It should be fun. Have a party and they will want to join in.

### What are some of the most common mistakes people make?

Taking a speaking brief at face value is a common mistake – be especially wary of the autocratic boss who says 'this is what they want'. Ideally, try and speak directly to some of the other people in the organisation – especially the troublemakers! And too many speakers never manage to get the audience on their side

### What are some of the less obvious problems you've encountered in your presentations or seen in others?

Small name badges can cause a problem where the names are so small that they can't be read by the presenter. It's important to address people by name. As Max Miller once said 'you honour the audience by honouring the individual'.

### How should you stand or move on stage during a presentation?

Movement is very important but it must be movement with a purpose. And never, ever walk up and down with your hands behind your back like a waiter. Movement which adds emphasis or brings extra life to a demonstration is something I do a lot.

### When you're at a panel discussion, how should you sit? Where should you look?

As another great comedian, Bob Monkhouse, said: 'you are always on show so you must be the first to react – to laugh, smile or nod. You are still performing at all times and you are being paid to give that performance.

### What is effective eye contact?

Genuine eye contact with members of the audience really helps you to generate rapport … staring into the distance or merely scanning the audience will lose that rapport. Staring at an individual might just win you a punch on the nose.

### Should you smile during your presentation?

That depends a lot on your personality. Because fun is such an important learning tool, I laugh and smile a lot. Let me put it this way: all other things being equal – same content same price same delivery – who would you rather hire, the person who smiled occasionally or the person who looks miserable?

### What do you do when someone asks a long question that never seems to end, or wants to ask more questions or engage with you when you've already answered them once?

Sometimes humour can rescue you. You say something like 'I had hair and teeth when that question started.' I will also say something like 'Let me answer the first part of that question now and perhaps we can take the rest of it offline afterwards.'

### What kinds of notes do you use?

Mostly I don't like to use any notes at all. Having a piece of paper in your hand is a major distraction for you and your audience – especially if it's shaking with fear. Sometimes I use visual aids – but sparingly. I try to divide my attention equally between my content and the audience. There isn't much RAM left over to deal with apparatus.

### Do you use PowerPoint in your presentations? (Give reasons)

Sometimes I use PowerPoint – more as an occasional prompt to myself than additional content for the audience. Mostly I would rather that they focus their attention on me.

I do, however, use PowerPoint extensively to prepare follow up presentations and supplementary material for course delegates.

# Jessica Arnold: Product Manager, Microsoft Corp.

*Jessica Arnold is a Product Manager at Microsoft Office (which includes PowerPoint, Word, Outlook, Excel and other programmes, depending on the version used).*

### What are some characteristics of an effective PowerPoint presentation?

I think the most effective presentations I've seen are the ones with the fewest slides. It's a question of getting the essential info on screen, of extrapolating the key ideas. You don't want a long series of bulleted slides, where the viewer has to read through every bullet. The most engaging presentations are the ones that are focused on the speakers and on the additional information and stories they have to tell.

### If you were to put together a half-hour presentation, how many slides would you use?

For a half-hour, I'd probably put together about three slides. It's not about using a bunch of slides and jamming a ton of information on each one. It's about focusing on the larger point, putting the high-level info on each slide and talking about it. That's the style that we use at Microsoft, and it seems to work really well.

With these long PowerPoint presentations, you get to a point where you just can't digest any more slides. A person can only look at so much on a screen; at some point, you need person-to-person interaction. If you can't get the information from a person, you might as well read it yourself in a document.

### What are some of the qualities of not-so-effective presentations?

They're usually very text heavy. When I put together a presentation, I ask myself this question: If I wasn't in the room, would my audience be getting the same content? If they could read it all themselves, you might as well just send it to them.

### How has Microsoft responded to criticisms that PowerPoint leads presenters to focus more on form than content, and that it's hard for viewers to decipher a central message?

Yes, I've heard those. They really have to do more with the way people have been using it, not the way we've ever suggested they use it. The idea that people should put together just a few slides and highlight a central message is not a shift in our approach at Microsoft.

Because of PowerPoint's sophisticated functionality, I think many people started using the programme to create complex documents that were meant to be printed, not delivered. Those are two different kinds of documents and, when it comes to making good documents versus good presentations, people have gotten confused along the way. The best practices for documents to be read are not the same as for effective presentations. For presentations, documents really need to be high impact and dynamic. At Microsoft, we take that to heart and do our best to give people the tools they need to create those kinds of presentations.

### What are some of the things we can expect with future versions of PowerPoint?

Our teams have been doing a lot of research, watching customers to see how people use the programme, what works and what doesn't. We've been evolving the programme to make sure it's user-friendly and provides the functionality people need for the way they use it today. As I mentioned, PowerPoint is not only being used to deliver presentations, but also to create a variety of sophisticated documents, like financial reports, scientific documents and documents of a sensitive nature that require certain read-only restrictions. That's a shift. They're linking tables, linking charts, emailing sensitive PowerPoint documents around to each other. We need to make sure that the programme stays up to par with all the different ways people use it.

# Presentation
## Resources

## Online Sources

### Microsoft Office Online

**http://office.microsoft.com**

Click 'PowerPoint' under Products in the left navigation bar to reach the Power-Point homepage, which provides access to animated tutorials, articles, free templates and other information on the software programme.

### Presentation Helper

**www.presentationhelper.co.uk**

PowerPoint templates and information on the alternatives to the Microsoft software join forces at this set of free resources for the first-time presenter.

### The Online Presenters Club

**http://www.ecademy.com/module. php?mod=club&c=2979**

Part of the business networking site Ecademy, this group aims to support individuals who may be nervous of presenting to overcome their fears and build on their skills.

### University of Newcastle Upon Tyne

**http://lorien.ncl.ac.uk/ming/dept/Tips/ present/present.htm**

Chiefly aimed at chemical engineers, this site has links to a number of articles aimed at individuals wanting to achieve extra clarity in their communication and presentation skills.

## Books

*Beyond Bullet Points: Using Microsoft PowerPoint to Create Presentations That Inform, Motivate and Inspire.*

**Atkinson, Cliff.**
**Microsoft Press, 2005. £24.99**

*PowerPoint Advanced Presentation Techniques.*

**Wempen, Faithe.**
**John Wiley & Sons, 2004. £39.99**

## Royalty-free clip art and photos

### Audio

**www.findsounds.com**

**www.freeaudioclips.com**

**wavplanet.com**

**wavsource.com**

## Images

**www.bigfoto.com**

**www.corbis.com**

**www.freefoto.com**

**www.geekphilosopher.com**

**www.jupiterimages.com**

**www.office.microsoft.com**

## Video

**www.animationfactory.com**

**www.freestockfootage.com**

# Index

# Acknowledgments

**The Planning Shop would like to thank:**

For their invaluable assistance as experts on a wide range of topics relating to presentations, PowerPoint and effective business communication:

Dr. Arnie Abrams, Professor, Applied Multimedia, Southern Oregon University (www.arnieabrams.net ); Jessica Arnold, Product Manager, Microsoft Office; Jean-luc 'JL' Doumont, JL Consulting (www.jlconsulting.be); Patricia Fripp, CSA, CSAE, (www.fripp.com); Mark Sanborn, Past National President, National Speakers Association (www.marksanborn.com); Katherine Wait, Senior Manager, Internet Services, Blue Shield of California.

**Rhonda Abrams would like to thank:**

Julie Vallone, who brought her constant professionalism, expert writing skills, easy-going personality and good humour to this project. Julie has been an outstanding addition to The Planning Shop team and we look forward to a long working relationship with her.

Dawne Bernhardt, who was my speaking coach years ago and whose lessons remain with me. Dawne taught me about the 'rule of three' and the 'mushy middle'. Thank you, Dawne!

Mireille Majoor, our Editorial Project Manager, who oversaw the development of this book and manages the editorial process of the entire line of books from The Planning Shop. She is a consummate professional and our books and readers have benefited from Mireille's commitment to excellence.

Arthur Wait, who designs the look and feel of everything carrying The Planning Shop name. We are always amazed (though no longer surprised) at the range of Arthur's talents and skills.

Diana Van Winkle, who brought her graphic expertise to improving and refining the design of this book. Her responsiveness and professionalism survived her move from Silicon Valley to Iowa, and we wish her well out there on the prairie.

Deborah Kaye, who manages The Planning Shop's relations with the academic community and who keeps us all together. She is our 'glue' and guiding light.

Dorienne Goodmanson, the newest member of The Planning Shop team, who's been an outstanding addition. Welcome, Dorienne!

Kathryn Dean, who brought her eagle eye to the editing and proofing process and creating the index in record time.

Finally, thanks to the three amazing dogs at The Planning Shop: Cosmo, Ozzy and Nana. Woof!

**Julie Vallone would like to thank:**

My daughter, Siena, for spilling juice on my keyboard when it was clearly time for a writer's break; our cats, Zoe, Squinky, Lola and Sappho, for keeping my feet and pages warm; and my husband Rick, for patiently putting up with the stacks of disheveled paper and books, scattered energy bar wrappers and thirty-four used coffee cups littering our dining table as deadline approached. And thanks to Mom, Dad, Nano and Pico for the extra babysitting.